The New Sustainable House

The New Sustainable House

Planet-friendly home design

PENNY CRASWELL

Previous spread: At
Regenerative Life Studio
in Japan, raised decks above
the house's foundations allow
nature to flourish undisturbed.

Opposite: A small house
clad in burnt timber in the
New Zealand forest.

Contents

Introduction

There is no one quick fix to sustainable architecture. My 2023 book, *Reclaimed: New homes from old materials*, explored how reclaimed, recycled and reconstituted materials are being used in new homes. Building on this, *The New Sustainable House* examines a multitude of ways that buildings can be made more environmentally friendly. It features 25 architect-designed homes from around the world that each have at least one sustainable design feature — many have several.

These projects show that, when it comes to house construction, the way things have always been done is not always the best way. No building is truly good for the environment — the construction industry is one of the most polluting industries in the world. Not being sustainable is the easier path. As one existing-materials consultancy in Melbourne spraypainted on its wall: 'Unsustainable is cheaper, unsustainable is faster, unsustainable is easier'. We all need to think outside the box and consider better solutions — clients, architects and builders.

The effort to build homes in a more sustainable way started more than half a century ago. Different approaches are taken in different parts of the world, but European countries, especially those further north where temperatures can get very cold, are world leaders in sustainable architecture. Many of their innovative solutions are now being adopted around the world.

The Passive House standard, developed in Sweden and Germany in 1988, is one such innovation. It is a voluntary standard for energy efficiency in a building. A certified Passive House must meet specific heating, cooling and energy demands, as well as criteria around airtightness and thermal comfort. This model is applied across Europe and is starting to be used in North America and Australasia. In the UK, the focus has been on renovating existing houses rather than building new ones and carbon calculators are being used to determine the carbon impact of building projects. In warmer climates, such as Mexico and Indonesia, different approaches are required for considerations like the orientation of buildings and the need for ventilation. Built-up areas, especially in Asia, require greening of the cities.

While going completely off-grid might seem like an easy way to ensure a sustainable house, it is not always possible or practical. And, when it comes to discarding solar panels and batteries at the end of their life, it may not even be the most environmentally friendly solution. There are many ways to introduce sustainability into the design and construction of your new home.

Sustainable design starts with the location of the project. Renovating, extending and retrofitting, including the adaptive reuse of old buildings, is always preferable to building a new structure. Building on empty land, either as urban infill or in less built-up areas, is always preferable to the demolition of existing buildings. Building small saves resources — both material and energy.

Next is the setting: architecture should not harm the natural environment. Options such as pile foundations and soil treatments preserve the existing land. Greenery can be added with rooftop and vertical gardens, and indoor plants.

Architects must also be responsive to the climatic conditions and use passive design principles where possible. 'Passive design' takes advantage of natural sources for heating, cooling, ventilation and lighting, reducing both the building's energy consumption and its carbon footprint. 'Active design' has the same goal, but uses technological solutions, such as solar panels and heat-recovery ventilation systems, to achieve it.

Then there's power: improvements in solar photovoltaic (PV) systems and battery storage are making energy production more environmentally friendly. Energy can also be sourced from hydronic (or radiant) heating, geothermal heat pumps or heat-recovery systems. However, in some cases, being connected to a grid that already uses renewable resources can be a better solution.

Water tanks or natural sources can be used to collect water, either for drinking or for toilets and gardens. Treating grey and black water on site is also ideal for protecting the environment.

New materials for sustainable design include bamboo at Echo House in Bali.

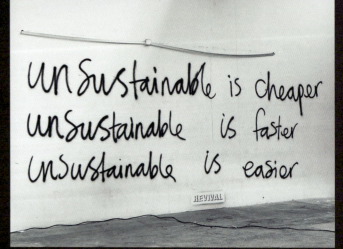

Following Passive House guidelines is another way to make a house truly sustainable. In most climates, energy-efficient houses are designed to be insulated and airtight, while also being breathable. Adhering to strict Passive House standards ensures a house's internal temperature is consistent and comfortable, with minimal leakage. When used in conjunction with a heat-recovery ventilation system, which also creates excellent indoor air quality, there can be almost no need for heating and cooling, even in extreme temperatures.

Another big consideration is material choice. When it comes to choosing materials for a new home, there are many factors that may affect the environment. Consider how far the material has travelled (to limit carbon emissions during transport), its thermal mass or insulating properties, and if it has been used before. New engineered timbers, such as cross-laminated timbers and prefabricated components, are good for the environment and also save time and waste on site. Reclaimed or salvaged materials, such as bricks and timber, and materials made from recycled waste, such as plastic and fabric, are ideal. Biomaterials (made from plants) and geomaterials (made from soil or earth) are also excellent sustainable choices. Finally, consider how easy it will be to disassemble and reuse or recycle the materials at the end of the building's life.

In 2022, a group of architects, designers and interior designers in the UK wrote an open letter to the UK design media, calling for it to up its game and stop publishing 'mainly flashy, resource-intensive projects'. Two years later, Australian builder Matthew Carland published an open letter on Instagram calling for Australian architects to do the same: 'Clients are demanding it, the planet is demanding it, and builders are demanding it. So, architects and designers, this one is on you.'

These examples highlight how much architects, clients, builders (and, to a lesser extent, the media) rely on each other to work together to make architecture more sustainable. Ideally, we are all on the same page, but, within each of these groups, there are those who are progressive, those who are apathetic — and everyone in-between. If we come together as allies in sustainable design, just think what we can achieve.

Designing with the environment in mind is not 'new'. What is new is the number of ways in which our houses can be made sustainable. No longer tied to one approach or a particular 'look', sustainability itself is an expanding topic. And if we are to challenge the old ways and protect our tiny, beautiful, blue planet, the time to act is right now.

List of terms

While this book is about sustainable house design, I have found that architects are using the term 'sustainable' less often than they used to. This may just be a shift in language, or perhaps it is to avoid accusations of 'greenwashing'. Instead, they tend to use specific terms — 'Passive House' or 'off grid' — or specific technologies — solar PV or heat-recovery ventilation systems.

Active design Design principles that reduce the need for energy use through technological solutions such as solar panels and heat-recovery systems (*see* Passive design).

Adaptive reuse The renovation of an existing building to give it a new life with a different use — usually from commercial to residential.

Biomaterials Building materials derived from biological ingredients, such as plants.

Biophilic design Design that connects people to nature, gardens and plants.

Carbon capture The ability of materials to sequester and store carbon.

Carbon neutral Carbon-dioxide emissions are reduced and balanced so that the net carbon footprint is neutral over time.

Circular design The idea that all products, including building materials, should be made from existing materials and reused at end of life.

Climate crisis/climate change Environmental changes, including air and land pollution, that threaten all life on Earth.

CO_2-controlled mechanical ventilation A ventilation system that modifies airflow on the basis of occupancy and activity in the room, measured as carbon dioxide.

Cross-laminated timber (CLT) An engineered timber made of at least three layers of timber arranged at right angles to one another and glued together.

Earth block construction A construction method that uses earth that has been compressed into strong, structural and durable blocks.

Embodied carbon The amount of carbon emissions associated with making or manufacturing a material, or designing and constructing a building.

Embodied energy The amount of energy it takes to make or manufacture a material.

Energy efficiency A measure of how much energy it takes to heat and cool a building.

Envelope The layer around the interiors of a building, which may be insulated and airtight or leaky and inefficient.

Forest Stewardship Council (FSC) An international not-for-profit body that certifies timbers and promotes responsible management of the world's forests.

G-value A measure of how much solar energy (heat from the sun's rays) is transmitted through a window. In cooler climates, a higher G-value is beneficial, as it reduces the need for heating.

Geomaterials Materials made from earth (e.g. rammed earth), including but not limited to waste earth.

Heat pump Because it extracts heat from a source, then amplifies and transfers the heat to where it is needed, a heat pump generates less greenhouse gas emissions than alternatives.

Heat-recovery ventilation system A mechanical system that delivers fresh, filtered air into a house while recovering thermal energy from the air.

Hemp A fast-growing crop that can be used to create hempcrete or other building materials. Hemp construction sequesters carbon dioxide, meaning it absorbs harmful emissions.

High performance A building that does not need a lot of heating or cooling due to its design.

Hydronic heating A heating system that circulates heated water or coolant through the home via pipes, often under the floor.

Indoor air quality The healthiness of the air, often improved by ventilation systems.

Kilowatt (kW) A unit of measurement for the rate of power an electrical device or load uses.

Kilowatt-hour (kWh) A unit of energy — 1 kWh is the amount of energy used by a 1000 watt appliance in one hour.

Lime mortar and plaster Lime mortar is used between bricks as an alternative to cement mortar. Lime plaster is used to finish a wall or ceiling as an alternative to gypsum or clay plaster. Lime is hydraulic, meaning it draws moisture out of the building, making it breathable and controlling humidity naturally.

Low energy A building that does not need to use a lot of energy to keep it at a comfortable temperature.

Low waste A renovation or new build that does not produce a lot of rubbish for landfill.

Net zero see Carbon neutral

Off grid A home that does not rely on a connection to standard utilities and infrastructure such as electricity, gas, water and sewerage.

Oriented strand board (OSB) A building product made by compressing layers of thin, rectangular wooden strips in specific orientations and bonding them with wax and adhesives.

Passive design Design principles that reduce the need for energy use through strategies such as the orientation of a house and the placement of openings, shading and ventilation (see Active design).

Passive House An international design standard that sets performance targets for insulation, airtightness, ventilation and heat recovery to deliver healthy, comfortable and efficient buildings. A building that complies with specific criteria set by the Passive House Institute can receive official certification.

Phase-change insulation Made of salts or waxy/oily organic compounds, phase-change materials absorb or release heat in the process of melting or freezing, providing thermal insulation to houses.

PHIUS certification This is the most common Passive House certification in the USA. See 'Passive House' for more information.

Post and beam foundations This type of foundation elevates houses above the earth, meaning there is less disruption to the natural environment than there is from digging and pouring a concrete slab. Also called pier and beam foundations.

Prefabrication (Prefab) Building components that are manufactured off site, then transported and assembled on site.

Radiant heating Rather than heating the air, a radiant heating system supplies heat directly to the floor or to panels in the walls or ceilings of a house.

Rain bioretention system A system that collects stormwater run-off and filters it using natural materials such as soil, plants and microbes before slowly releasing it.

Reclaimed/recycled materials Materials that have been salvaged from building sites or elsewhere and reused, or that make use of recycled waste, including post-consumer waste.

Regenerative architecture An architectural style that results in a benefit to the ecosystem.

Retrofit To fit insulation and/or create airtight seals to an existing building to increase its energy efficiency.

Shou sugi ban A traditional Japanese technique of charring the surface of wood with fire.

Shower heat-recovery unit A system that reclaims heat from used water that would otherwise go down the drain, and uses it to heat incoming cold water.

Small footprint An apartment or house with a small floor area, which uses fewer materials and less energy to build and run.

Solar PV system Photovoltaic (PV) cells convert sunlight into electricity. Multiple PV cells are connected to form a single solar panel, and multiple solar panels can be connected to form an array, which is usually installed on the roof of the home. An inverter converts the power generated by the PV panels into a current that can be used in the home. Unused power can be sent to the electrical grid by the inverter, or stored in a battery.

Structural Insulated Panel System (SIPS) A panel with two outer layers, usually oriented strand board, and an inner layer of insulating material.

Thermal-bridge free A construction technique that focuses on minimising the number of areas where heat is lost in a building. A thermal bridge is a location with less insulation.

Thermally broken window frames A type of window frame with a non-metallic resin or plastic material that physically separates the interior part of the window from the exterior part, reducing heat transfer.

U-value A measure of how much heat is transferred through a window. The lower the value, the better the insulation properties of the window.

Wood burner with wetback water heater A wetback system can be attached to wood, pellet, coal or diesel burners. The heat from the fire is used to heat water.

Below: Cross-laminated timber
was used as a structural
material in Svinninge Cabin
in Sweden.

Right: Weave House in India
is an off-grid home with solar
power and water tanks.

Green house in the city

PROJECT	19 Waterloo Street
LOCATION	Sydney, New South Wales, Australia
ARCHITECT	SJB
LANDSCAPE	Dangar Barin Smith
BUILDER	Promena Projects
SITE AREA	30 m²
BUILDING AREA	27 m²
FLOOR AREA	69 m²
STOREYS	3
PHOTOGRAPHY	Anson Smart

A roof garden adds green space
to this new home on a tiny
and under-utilised city plot.

SUSTAINABLE FEATURES

Battery
Green roof
Heat pump
Heat-recovery ventilation system
Reclaimed bricks
Reclaimed timber floors
Solar (2.5 kW PV array)
Wood fire

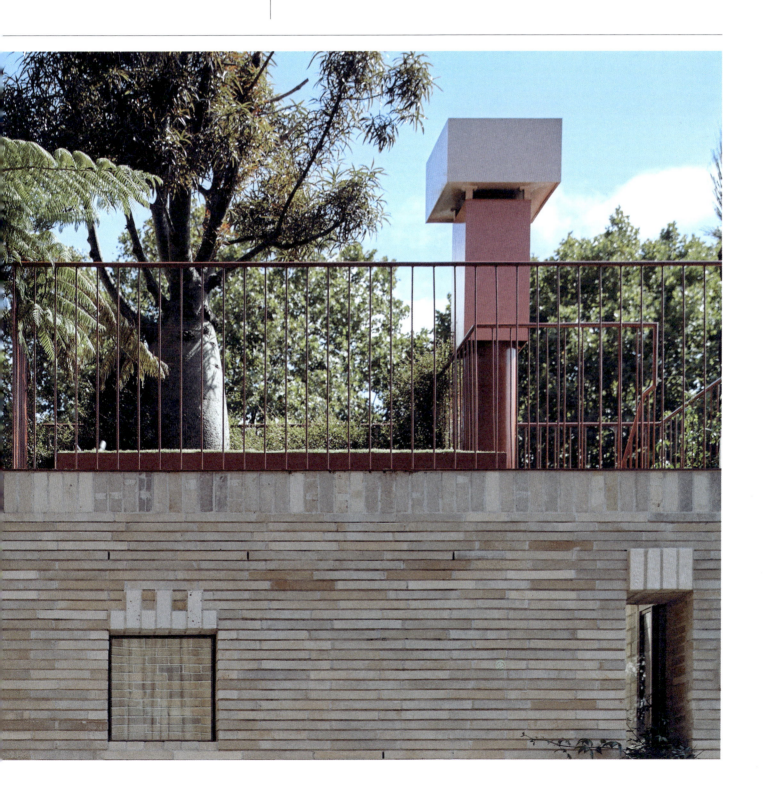

This house was designed not to create more space but to go smaller. Architect Adam Haddow from SJB built the home in an empty backyard in the centre of Sydney. It is a long, skinny house with an intentionally small footprint, equipped with solar and battery power, a heat-recovery ventilation system, a heat pump for hot water, a green roof, reclaimed timber inside and a reclaimed brick facade.

When Adam bought it, the property contained a mixed retail shop in front, a residential home behind and a concrete backyard. It was ripe for reinvention, offering a chance to add density to the city while creating liveable small spaces. The site is now split into three parts — at the front is a renovated house with a small commercial space downstairs and a two-bedroom apartment upstairs, but behind this is where the real innovation happened. In what used to be the backyard of the old terrace there is now a completely new and charmingly lopsided three-storey home built from reclaimed brick.

The most striking element of the design of the house is the facade. It was inspired by the mismatched, asymmetrical townhouse in one of Adam's favourite films, *Mon Oncle*. At 19 Waterloo Street, the windows and doors are dotted here and there — some square, rectangular, arched or round, at different heights, some large, some small — to create the same charming effect. There are also red metal elements — a gate and oblique windows at ground level —that add to the look.

The bricks are rejects from another project. Adam came across them by chance at a brickyard. At the time, he wasn't sure where he could use them, but knew they shouldn't go to waste. 'Lots of them had been broken in transit going up and coming back. They couldn't sell them and were just going to crush them up for road base,' he says. As it turns out, they were perfect for creating the facade, and the broken bricks were also used for decorative effect, alongside a new white-glazed brick.

At less than 30 square metres, the footprint of this house is very small. On both sides of the building, half-mezzanine-level steps lead to three large rooms on the east and four smaller rooms on the west — a total of seven split levels. At ground level, the entry opens to a combined study/library with oblique windows to the street.

A staircase with a leather-clad banister takes you upstairs, where corridors are lined in brick and timber. On the first level, the kitchen, in one of the smaller rooms, has brick floors, timber ceilings, and joinery in stainless steel with bright handles in geometric shapes that echo the arched window and a tiny red shutter window that opens to the street.

Opposite the kitchen is the largest room of the house, a living room with minimal furnishings, including a built-in mustard corduroy couch and a bouclé armchair, a wood fire and access to a small courtyard garden with green walls and a tall tree. Like the kitchen, this room has brick floors and timber ceilings. It is dominated by a huge landscape painting by Sydney artist Nicholas Harding that shows the local landscape as it would have looked before colonisation.

Upstairs, there is a walk-in wardrobe and a bathroom stacked on the smaller side of the house, both in burgundy wine colours. The bathroom features a vanity in the same marble as the floor, which also wraps up to create a ledge in the shower. The shower is large, designed for two, and has a circular skylight overhead and lush green planting behind. The richness of the burgundy tiles on the walls is complemented by timber taps, designed by Adam, that tilt to turn on and form a circle when off. On the top level of the home is the bedroom. Arched and rectangular windows puncture the walls, and the burgundy theme continues in the bedhead and carpet.

Incredibly, the rooftop garden features a mature bottle tree along with the other garden and courtyard plants. Its existence on the roof seems a minor miracle, considering its size in relation to the house. Other plants were chosen to improve passive cooling and biodiversity for the neighbourhood. There are solar panels on the roof of the apartment next door, and battery storage that provides 90 per cent of the energy consumption for all three spaces. The house also has old-fashioned solutions to keep heating and cooling costs down, like the awning to the main living room that creates shade when needed.

The architects used some Passive House principles in the installation of internal insulation and a heat-recovery ventilation system, which is great for city air and pollen, but chose not to make the house airtight. 'It's not 100 per cent a Passive House, because Sydney is quite different to northern Europe. Some of the principles around Passive House are amazing, but they probably don't directly translate,' says Adam. 'We do want a bit of leakiness in our houses sometimes, and other times you want to close them down.'

This project is the result of a way of thinking that discards the obvious solution in favour of a more intellectual response to the problems of urban sprawl, the contribution of construction to harmful landfill and our reliance on fossil fuels. All in all, this house is a comfortable and joyful home for the architect and his small family, as well as representing a sustainable approach to city living.

The main living room opens onto
a tiny garden that has a tall
tree and painted green walls.

Top: The kitchen cupboards have colourful geometric handles.

Middle: In the kitchen, custom timber taps open by tilting sideways.

Bottom: The living room is dominated by *Eora*, a painting of pre-settlement Sydney by Nick Harding.

Opposite: The kitchen has low ceilings and stainless-steel finishes, plus one arched and one square window.

Left: The bathroom features burgundy tiles, marble, lush greenery and a round skylight.

Right: The bedroom is on the top floor, with Pierre Frey—embroidered linen curtains.

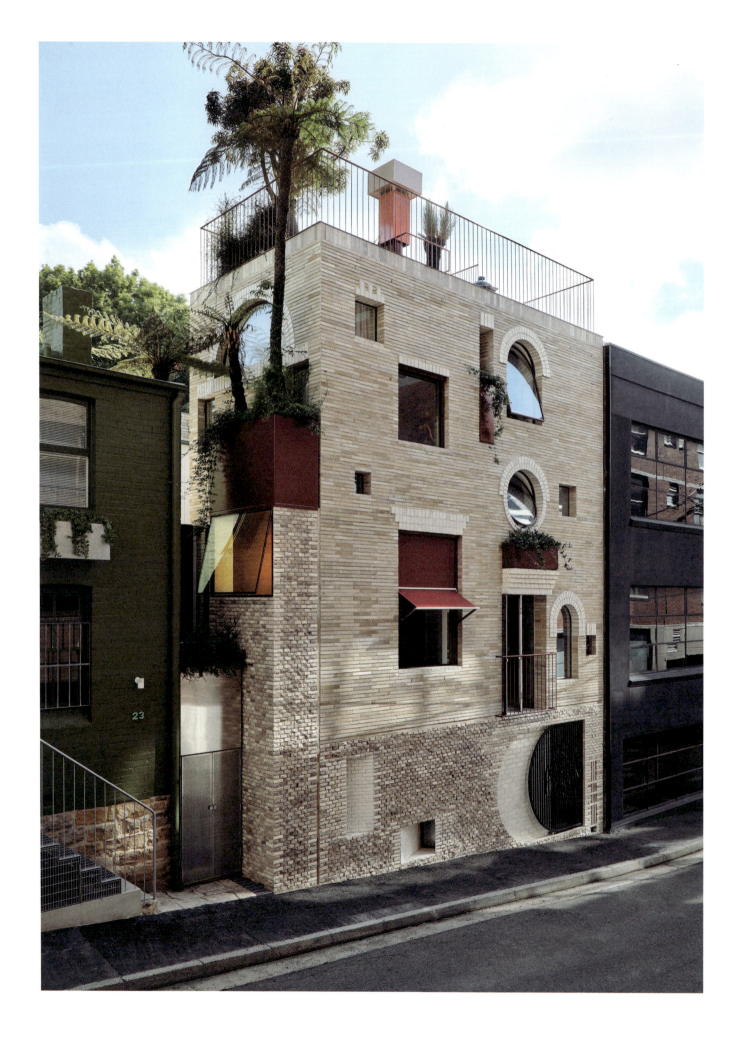

Left: The facade of the house uses bricks reclaimed from another project.

Below: The hardy, drought-tolerant Queensland bottle tree is part of a mission to green the city.

GREEN ROOF

The benefits of being in nature are manifold. Biophilia — a love of nature — means we feel less stress, more joy, calmer and more creative, and can breathe better when we spend time in gardens. Rooftop gardens help cool urban environments and improve air quality and biodiversity, including offering habitats for bees and other pollinators. And importantly, they increase the energy efficiency of buildings by removing heat from the air through the process of evapotranspiration, and by acting as insulators for buildings.

Even small rooftops, such as the one at 19 Waterloo Street, can have a big impact. SJB worked with landscape design studio Dangar Barin Smith to create this particular garden, whose centrepiece is a Queensland bottle tree. Getting such a mature tree up into this small space was a challenge, and it had to be tied into its spot until its roots took hold, but it has been a complete success. The tree also creates a canopy so the rooftop garden can be enjoyed even in midsummer. The roof garden at 19 Waterloo Street also lowers the urban heat island effect while adding to a network of urban gardens across the city.

Back to fundamentals

PROJECT	Minimum House
LOCATION	Toyota, Aichi Prefecture, Japan
ARCHITECT	Nori Architects
BUILDER	TOKORO
SITE AREA	138 m²
BUILDING AREA	50 m²
FLOOR AREA	88 m²
STOREYS	2
PHOTOGRAPHY	Jumpei Suzuki

This Japanese home, made with low-cost, functional materials, is airtight with high levels of thermal comfort.

SUSTAINABLE FEATURES

Airtight construction
Exterior insulation
Grade 3 earthquake rating
Soil treatment
Unfinished structural materials

Designed for a young family in the city of Toyota, about an hour from Nagoya, Japan, Minimum House transforms structural and insulation materials into interior and exterior finishes to create a highly efficient building with a unique appearance. It was designed by Nori Architects as a prototype of high-performance, low-cost architecture made with fewer materials.

This is the least expensive house that Nori Architects has ever designed. The challenge led Nori Kawashima to ask how much of a house could be subtracted while maintaining maximum energy performance. '[I] considered "What are the non-negotiables in housing?"' he explains. 'I decided that, in addition to structural safety, thermal comfort and energy conservation, a modern urban residence should be open to the inside and outside, and to nature — sun and wind.'

With this mission in mind, the house was designed as a compact box over two storeys. The site has heavy traffic to the west and close neighbours to the north and south, so the house was built with a small courtyard facing a smaller street to the east. On this side of the home, at the entrance, is a covered terrace with galvanised wire mesh and translucent folded plates. These permeable materials allow light and air through into the house, while maintaining privacy from the street. Large windows on the second level of the south-eastern facade provide access to winter sun as well as views of the neighbourhood. On the top floor, a mesh-enclosed balcony outside the bedroom, made of a steel pallet rack, overlooks the garden.

The interiors are split over two storeys and a mezzanine. On the ground floor is the built-in kitchen, dining and storage space — this room is also connected to an outdoor terrace for warm weather. Behind the kitchen is tucked the bathroom, the washing machine and a large multipurpose room. Up the timber stairs, on the second floor, large windows to the south and east overlook the smaller street. Here, long sheer curtains can be pulled for privacy and there is another toilet hidden on this level. On the top floor, stacked above the kitchen, are two bedrooms, one of which has the potential to be divided into two children's rooms in future. The main bedroom opens out to the balcony.

The interiors are mostly clad in a structural timber, without additional finishes. This reduction in materials is part of the ethos of the design. The plywood walls, ceilings, floors and stairs are structural, and the plumbing piping and electrical wiring are all exposed. Built-in furniture, including shelving, window seats and kitchen islands, plus tables, chairs and other elements, are all also in wood. 'Traditionally, wood has been used extensively in construction in Japan, but it is not necessarily common in recent years,' explains Nori.

The house has exterior insulation in the form of a phenolic foam board, plus high-performance window sashes and eaves that ensure the building is airtight. Testing has measured the level of airtightness, and the home performed above the energy conservation standard. Earthquake resistance was also achieved by placing load-bearing walls with structural plywood and steel braces at appropriate intervals, while suppressing deformation and ensuring spatial flexibility. A comfortable thermal environment for the interiors was achieved at low cost by creating ventilation routes, and using fans and ducts to distribute warm/cold air from an underfloor air conditioner.

The soil of the site was regenerated by digging trenches and filling them with straw, charcoal and fallen leaves, then placing a layer of crushed stones and wood chips on top. This allows water and air to move through the soil throughout the site. The materials were provided by farmers, and construction was carried out in a workshop by the home's owner, the builder, designers and university students. Saplings were planted in the backyard, along with fruiting trees and herbs to fill out the garden.

The holistic approach to sustainable architecture in this low-cost, low-waste, environmentally friendly and energy-efficient house has made it a benchmark project. If the devil is in the details, then this house's attention to every aspect of its environment, from the air right down to the soil, puts it out front.

Below: The ground floor has
a dining room and kitchen,
and behind those, a bathroom,
laundry and multipurpose room.

Following page: Interior
finishes have been omitted,
leaving the wooden structure
of the house exposed.

MATERIAL EFFICIENCY

When talking about sustainable design features, it's easy to forget that one of the most sustainable construction methods is to simply reduce materials — the very first part of the famous saying 'reduce, reuse, recycle'. Instead of interior finishes made from local, easily replaced, recycled or biobased materials, what if there were no finishes used at all? Structural elements like timber, steel and concrete can be beautiful without a plaster, veneer or paint finish.

At Minimum House, this philosophy has been taken to its extreme, bringing the use of materials down to the minimum and creating an efficient home whose aesthetic is determined by its structural and functional components. As well as exposing its structural timber, the ventilation fans and ducts, electric wires (bundled neatly together) and pipes are on full display, while the exterior shows its wire mesh and translucent panels. The resulting house has an unusual aesthetic, but the extensive use of natural timber makes it feel warm and inviting.

Above: Upstairs, the balcony has wire mesh and translucent panels, and a steel pallet rack underfoot.

Opposite: The second-floor living room has large windows and a translucent curtain for privacy.

Burnt timber meets earthy tones

PROJECT	Somers House
LOCATION	Mornington Peninsula, Victoria, Australia
ARCHITECT	Kennedy Nolan
BUILDER	Bartlett Architectural Construction
SITE AREA	2159 m²
BUILDING AREA	630 m²
FLOOR AREA	430 m²
STOREYS	3
PHOTOGRAPHY	Derek Swalwell

The timber cladding in the
recessed black facade was
burnt using *shou sugi ban*,
a technique that originated
in Japan.

SUSTAINABLE FEATURES

Hydronic floor heating
Phase-change roof insulation
Shou sugi ban
Solar (18.5 kW PV array)

This fully accessible, energy-efficient beach house on the Mornington Peninsula, south of Melbourne, was designed for a couple and their grown-up children and partners. The owners appointed architecture studio Kennedy Nolan to design a replacement for the dilapidated house they had used as a weekender for decades. As well as having problems including damp, poor ventilation and poor orientation, it was not set up to meet the needs of the owners, one of whom has a disability and needs an accessible house with wheelchair access. 'We are very circumspect about demolishing and starting again, but this one couldn't do what they needed it to do,' says architect Rachel Nolan. 'It was at the end of its life.'

The architects' response to the brief is an accessible, passively designed home that is oriented intelligently for the sun and climate, uses long-lasting local and natural materials, and has sustainable systems in place. One of the most outstanding features is the layout — it has been designed as three separate 'apartments', two of which can be closed off to save heating and cooling costs when not in use.

At the end of the driveway, which is slightly curved to make the approach to the house more protected, stands the new L-shaped building. The main part of the house is built parallel to the beach and a striking black-clad wing extends up the hill to the left. This almost unbroken black facade has a shallow arch with parking underneath. Made of a chemical-free modified timber, the facade has been burnt black in the Japanese *shou sugi ban* style to make it durable and reduce the need to maintain the finish over time. 'It is the most beautiful thing, like a dinosaur or a crocodile,' says Rachel. '[The timber] arrived, then they burnt every tongue and groove. It is a velvety, rich black backdrop.'

The main living quarters are on the middle level — one storey above ground — but can be accessed from the ground floor at the front of the house, due to the slope of the site. As well as a generous living, kitchen and dining space, plus a main bedroom suite, this level has wide circulation spaces for wheelchair use and a spacious bathroom with a sink designed to allow a wheelchair to fit underneath. Views of the garden and beach behind the house are uninterrupted by balconies or decks. This was important, especially for this client. Rachel explains that 'the house needs to hold her really comfortably, so she feels safe in it. She can see what's going on, but not necessarily be seen as well. Even if she can't get to the beach, she can see it.'

The guest apartment on the level below features a bedroom, bathroom and laundry, a living space (which is also perfect for physiotherapy), an outdoor dining space tucked under the house on one side and a sauna next to the bathroom at the other end.

The third apartment, also for guests, is in the wing that goes up the hill. Joined to the other part of the house by a central lift core that accesses all three levels, this wing was built on a previously disused part of the site and includes a carport and storeroom on the ground floor, and two living areas, two bedrooms and a bathroom on the level above.

Inside this home, the rich earthy colours were inspired by the paintings of Indigenous Gija artist Queenie McKenzie, and materials were chosen for longevity, including hardwood (rather than veneers) for the joinery. Other materials include stone, terracotta, cork, exposed concrete, wool and linen curtain fabrics, and brass tapware. It was important to use as few composite materials as possible so that everything can eventually be recycled.

The house was designed to maximise energy efficiency, with windows, facades and screens positioned to make the most of the winter sun and block the harsh western sun. 'The friction on this site is that the views are all south and north is up the hill. You want to look at the sea, but you want the sun from the north,' says Rachel. This was managed by double glazing to the north and triple glazing to the south, plus the installation of insulation, including phase-change material in the roof. A thermal chimney expels hot air in summer and captures south-west winds. There are solar panels on the roof, an electric car charger and an underground rainwater tank that collects water for the toilets and landscaping. The hot water and hydronic heating are powered by an electric heat pump.

This warm and inviting house makes the most of a complex brief, with passive design principles, long-lasting materials and sustainable systems supporting an architectural response that is ultimately about providing a comfortable and accessible home for a couple and their extended family.

The windows allow direct
views of the ocean,
uninterrupted by a balcony
or deck.

Top: The bathroom is spacious and the sink allows a wheelchair to fit underneath.

Middle: This corridor space features a totem sculpture from the Tiwi Islands.

Bottom: Shades of earthy pink and rust red combine with velvet upholstery and linen curtains to provide warmth.

Opposite: The fireplace is perfect for days when storms and cold weather prevail.

Previous page: The main
kitchen and dining space
features brass suspension
lamps by Paola Navone.

Above: The boat shed near
the beach has also been
refurbished.

Opposite: This living space,
with its ocean views and
northern light, is the most
used part of the house.

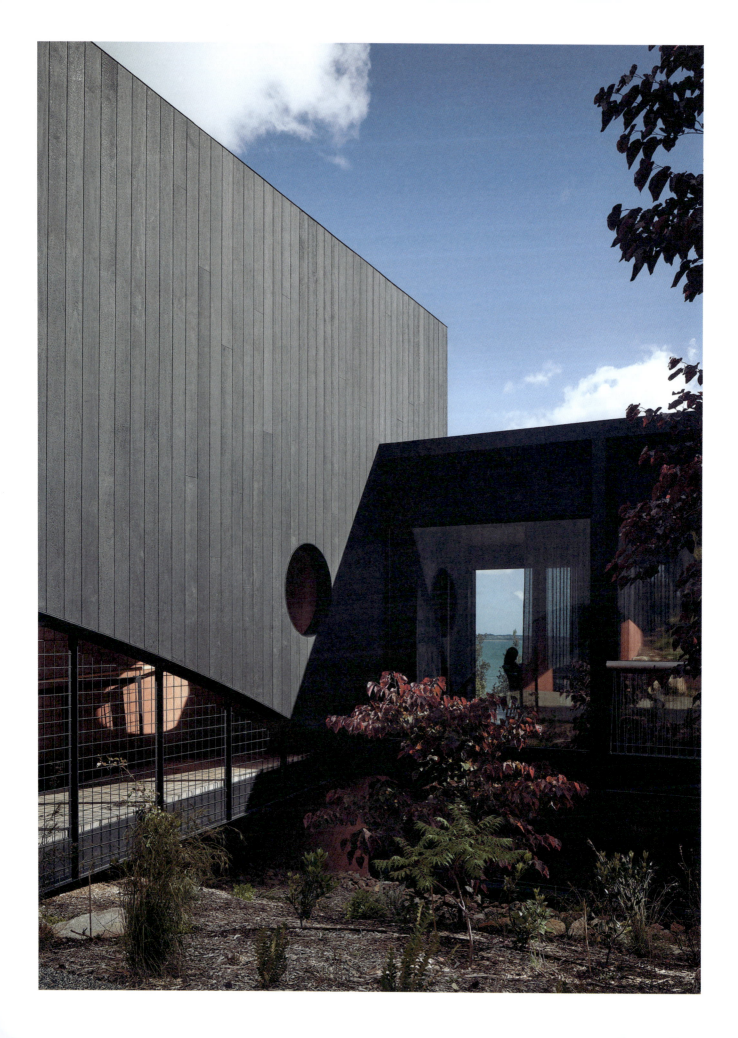

Opposite: This is the nexus between the main living and bedroom suite and the *shou sugi ban*-clad wing.

Below: Black exteriors are contrasted with bright colours inspired by Mexican architect Luis Barragán.

SHOU SUGI BAN

Shou sugi ban (also known as *yakisugi*) is a traditional Japanese technique of charring the surface of wood with fire. Among its many benefits are that burning the surface creates a black layer that protects the wood from termites and other insects, mould, water and fire. In addition, once the process is complete, it does not need refinishing or maintenance. *Shou sugi ban* has been used for centuries in Japan — some surviving examples date back as far as the 1600s.

The architects chose to clad Somers House in *shou sugi ban* for its durability and low-maintenance qualities, but also to create an aesthetic that was recessive in the landscape — they describe it as 'zoomorphic' or animal-like. The architects also appreciated its ability to withstand weather, insects and fire. The *shou sugi ban* was created with timber cladding that was burnt in a factory setting and touched up on site. The black, almost velvety appearance complements the ochre-toned exterior render patinated with tannins and salt.

Constructed from mud

PROJECT	Marfa Suite
LOCATION	Marfa, Texas, USA
ARCHITECT	DUST
BUILDER	E&C Construction
SITE AREA	1608 m²
BUILDING AREA	142 m²
STOREYS	1
PHOTOGRAPHY	Casey Dunn

The guest suite is made
of double-width compressed
earth block walls and has
an insulating air gap.

SUSTAINABLE FEATURES

Blown-in roof insulation
Earth block construction
Radiant underfloor heating
Underground rainwater basins

Arizona-based architecture studio DUST chose a traditional construction method to create a building that withstands the wild temperature swings of the desert climate. Located in the Texas town of Marfa, famous for its sparse emptiness and minimalist art movement, Marfa Suite is primarily made from compressed earth blocks. Their high thermal mass makes them an optimal solution for saving energy, especially in this climate.

The project began when DUST was approached by a family with a home in Marfa who needed more space. Rather than extend their existing home, a mud brick — or adobe — building designed by Rael San Fratello, they wanted to create a separate building for guests, or for the owners to use when guests were in the main house. In a nod to the main house, they decided to again use mud, this time in the form of compressed earth.

The decision to use earth blocks was inspired by the adobe structures found along the US–Mexican border — a style of building that was once ubiquitous but is becoming increasingly rare. In the 1970s there were more than 300 adobe yards in New Mexico; now there are only about nineteen. Adobe used to be common all the way from south Texas to California, the south-west border region and northern parts of Mexico. 'Anywhere there were Indigenous cultures and Spanish influence in that region,' explains architect Jesús Robles. 'It's a heritage that is being lost. Any project that is constructing out of earth in this region is sustaining and prolonging a way of building structures. It's not so much a performative but a cultural aspect or perspective on sustainability, which I think we feel as architects and builders we have a responsibility to maintain.'

The unique weather conditions of the Texan desert were also a major factor in the design. Houses here must deal with both the heat of the desert in summer and extreme cold — including ice and snow — in winter. There is also the diurnal swing — the temperature can oscillate wildly between hot days and cold nights. 'It's high desert,' explains Jesús, who spent his youth travelling between southern California and Texas. 'It cools down in the evening, so there's a bigger diurnal swing.'

The architects sourced local earth blocks that are highly compressed and have an insulating air gap. The mixture includes a little cement, meaning that, unlike traditional adobe, the finish does not have to be reapplied every few years, just sprayed with a penetrating sealant. The blocks perform well in the desert environment, and because they are made from local earth, blend in with the landscape. 'While we believe this project can last more than a century, if not longer, eventually it will return to the earth and become a remnant memory,' says architect Cade Hayes.

Although the new building only has one bedroom, one bathroom and one living space, and has no kitchen, it does not lack amenity. There is a built-in desk and bookshelves at one end of the living space, storage in the bedroom, a full bathroom with wet room, an outdoor dining room and even an outdoor shower. There are unspoiled views past the back deck towards the open plains of the Chihuahuan Desert, and a brick wall shields the guesthouse from the road. 'I think the main impetus was to build a place for them to occupy while they had guests but [also to design] a place they can work, lounge and live while being connected to the landscape and the gardens that they have curated,' says Cade.

The roof is designed to collect rainwater and deliver it to strategic locations on the property where trees and foliage have been planted to shade the building during the hottest time of the year. The water goes to underground basins on the north-east and north-west of the building. The house was initially designed so that it wouldn't need air conditioning, so although the clients ended up installing a system, it is not needed for much of the year. While the insulated roof does not yet have solar panels, it is designed to allow easy installation in future.

Sustainability is not just about protecting the environment. It can also be about protecting traditional methods of construction, like the adobe construction methods found in this part of the USA and Mexico. This project proves that, as well as creating enduring structures that sit comfortably in their environment, these traditional materials also have insulating properties that reduce the need for heating and cooling.

From the bathroom, a glazed
door opens to a private
outdoor shower.

Previous page: This compressed
earth block is finished with
a seal that can be resprayed
every three years.

Opposite: The concrete lintels
above the doors were cast
in place.

Right: A built-in desk
overlooks the garden and has
a view of Haystack Mountain
in the Chihuahuan Desert.

EARTH BLOCK

Adobe is a form of sun-dried brick construction traditionally used in Mexico and the US states of California, New Mexico, Arizona and Texas. Originally introduced by the Pueblo Indians in New Mexico and the Jumano and Apache Indians in Texas as early as the 1400s, it is both locally abundant and well adapted to the climate. It has a high thermal mass, absorbing and storing heat during the day and releasing it at night.

The architects did not use a traditional adobe construction for Marfa Suite, but instead chose a compressed earth block that has the advantage of being almost maintenance-free. While the use of earth-based materials is in decline in the region, this form of construction should be celebrated as an excellent sustainable solution for contemporary housing. Utilising earth-based construction also helps to support adobe production yards and keep Indigenous and Hispanic traditions alive.

Opposite: The suite was
designed for the owners
to use while visitors stay
in the main house.

Below: Grey concrete floors
complement the brown of
the compressed earth blocks.

Verdant off-grid retreat

PROJECT	Weave House
LOCATION	Surat, Gujarat, India
ARCHITECT	The B.A.D Studio
SITE AREA	6968 m²
BUILDING AREA	2415 m²
FLOOR AREA	604 m²
STOREYS	1
PHOTOGRAPHY	The Fishy Project, Noaidwin Studio

Designed as a holiday home,
Weave House allows the owners
to reconnect with nature.

SUSTAINABLE FEATURES

Biowaste fertiliser
Off grid
Solar (10 kW PV array)
Underground water tank (12 kL)

This new home was designed as a meditative weekend retreat and offers a chance to coexist with nature and embrace sustainable building design. Located on farmland in the village of Aamri, 35 kilometres from Surat, India, the house was designed by the Gujurat-based Bureau for Architecture and Design (B.A.D) Studio.

While sustainable architecture and design has been gaining traction in this part of India, partly thanks to subsidies for solar and wind projects, it was the COVID-19 pandemic that opened the eyes of many city dwellers to the importance of access to green vegetation. 'The post-COVID era made people realise how important nature is, especially when they were confined within city blocks,' explains architect Boney Keriwala.

The owners of Weave House had a boomerang-shaped site with an approach sparsely populated with trees and a far end lush with mango and sapodilla trees and a coconut plantation on the periphery. In response to a brief asking them to create a weekend home to rejuvenate the senses and connect with nature, the architects envisaged a house at the front part of the site and convinced the owners to invest in sustainable design systems. 'We started putting ideas to the client about how [sustainable features] can be beneficial to nature and him as well, and luckily he came on board with extensive enthusiasm,' says Boney.

The house consists of two main rectangular blocks: a brick one for public spaces and a concrete one for private rooms. The brick is a clay terracotta, sometimes used as a solid wall and sometimes perforated, depending on the need for privacy or cross-ventilation. Boney says the grey and neutral concrete is used to 'soothe the mind, body and soul'. Both materials are also finished with distinctive patterns inspired by the owner's background in textiles — Ikat print patterns on the terracotta brick and fabric threads on the concrete walls. 'On a macro level, it's a marriage of brick and concrete, and on a micro level, all those intricate fabrics have been interpolated onto the facade,' says Boney.

The site is a floodplain, around 400 metres from the Purna River, so the house is elevated to prevent waterlogging. The neighbourhood mainly consists of old rural houses interspersed with newly built homes. Each has a raised plinth with an *otta* (front veranda) that is used as a social space to interact with neighbours or as an extra space for festivities.

The entry to Weave House unfolds gradually, starting from the porch, leading via an enclosed hallway to an entry hall with a waiting bench made from reclaimed teak. The entry hall is connected to a main living room with two sitting spaces. The adjoining room features a dining room and open-plan kitchen plus an enclosed kitchen and wash area to the side. The private rooms are laid along the other side of the house — three bedrooms and three bathrooms — and there is a fourth bedroom at the north-eastern end of the house, next to the living space. The spatial planning, inspired by a traditional house, is modernised with design elements and materials to constitute a contemporary home woven into a rural settlement.

Between the two main parts of the house is an open-air courtyard with tropical planting and foliage that cascades from the roof. Small courtyards in the bathrooms bring in light and create an indoor-outdoor connection. The pool deck and swimming pool are screened by concrete and perforated brick walls that provide privacy while serving as an elegant backdrop for the surrounding flora. The home is built around the notion of coexisting with nature, allowing for smooth transitions and giving its occupants a tranquil retreat to unwind and connect with the outside world.

Thanks to its sustainable systems, the house is more or less self-sufficient. Solar panels on the roof supply enough power for the house's daily needs. A rainwater harvesting tank provides water for the site, with most of the run-off being absorbed in the ground through recharge pits, and the groundwater being re-pumped for gardening and orchards. The house's biodegradable waste is used to make biofertilisers for the organic garden, which the owners planted behind the house to grow their own food.

Rather than replacing or adding to an existing building, this house shows how new builds on uninhabited land can respect nature and provide a dwelling that has sustainable systems built in from the very start. Comfortable and built to last, this house creates a green sanctuary for its owners to enjoy for many decades to come.

Below: The internal courtyard
that runs through the centre
of the house is lined with
perforated brick screens.

Following page: The interiors
of the main living space are
grey and the walls are washed
in lime paints.

Top: The patterns on the terracotta brick are inspired by textile designs.

Middle: View from a bedroom to an external perforated brick wall screening the road.

Bottom: Each bathroom ends with a tiny, open air, outdoor garden.

Opposite: Floor-to-ceiling glazing in the dining room creates the illusion of being outdoors.

WATER TANKS

Harvesting rainwater in water tanks reduces a home's reliance on mains water, lowering water bills and minimising the effect of water restrictions put in place due to drought. In rural or remote locations, connecting to mains water may not be possible, but even when it is, rainwater can be used to water gardens, irrigate crops and fight fires. Using water tanks also reduces damage to the local environment, as excess water goes into the tanks rather than waterlogging the ground.

Weave House was designed around the flow of water through the site. Around 12,000 litres of rainwater are harvested annually in a large underground tank and used in the house and gardens, including the vegetable garden and orchards. Meanwhile, percolation pits on the edges of the site help to preserve the groundwater level.

Above: The pool is screened off, creating a tranquil oasis.

Opposite: The house is elevated to prevent waterlogging in times of flood.

Energy generator

PROJECT	Garden House
LOCATION	Melbourne, Victoria, Australia
ARCHITECT	Austin Maynard Architects
BUILDER	Sargant Construction
ENERGY CONSULTANT	Cundall
LANDSCAPING	Cheeky Nature Landscaping
INTERIOR STYLING	Simone Haag
SITE AREA	773 m²
BUILDING AREA	535 m²
STOREYS	2
PHOTOGRAPHY	Derek Swalwell

The wing that houses the garage and home office sits at the front of the block, on the footprint of the original house.

SUSTAINABLE FEATURES

80% recycled glass roof insulation
Batteries (2 x 26 kW)
Cavity slab insulation
Compost bin
Double-glazed windows
Double-thickness walls
Fly ash concrete

Heat pump
Heat-recovery ventilation system
Hydronic heating
Off grid
Recycled brick
Solar (17 kW PV array)
Thermally broken window frames
Underground water tanks (2 x 5 kL)

Garden House, in an inner-city suburb of Melbourne, is made up of three connected two-storey pavilions. Designed to make the most of the site and climate, the house is equipped with several sustainable systems and technologies, ultimately generating more energy than it uses. The owners are a young family who are passionate about sustainability (one is the CEO of a climate advocacy group). They were keen to make sure the house was 100 per cent electric, incorporating solar power, two electric batteries, a car charging station and as many other sustainable design ideas as possible.

Austin Maynard Architects could not have been a better choice for this particular mission. The practice includes sustainable design as a given on all their projects. The principals ascribe this to their Tasmanian roots and the fact that they both earned degrees in environmental design before completing their architecture degrees. As Andrew Maynard explains, '[Sustainable design] is the starting point for anybody who studied in Tassie so that's where every project starts for us.'

The first important decision was where to position the house on the site. The previous house was at the front of the block, which is long and narrow like its neighbours, with an untouched backyard that opens out behind. The best solution for the new house was to place one of the pavilions at the front and build the other two in the backyard.

The front pavilion has a garage, bike storage and a workshop plus a multipurpose room on the ground level and a home office on the second storey, all clad in white-coated metal. The second pavilion forms the main part of the new house. The ground floor features living, dining and kitchen spaces, and a pool, and the main bedroom suite is on the level above. In the third pavilion, at the back of the block, is the children's wing with a living space on the ground floor and bedrooms and a bathroom upstairs.

The house was positioned so there was no need to uproot any established trees. Even the footings of the house were designed to be sensitive to the garden and, in places, are suspended above the ground to protect structural tree root zones. The garden is an important part of the house. It is irrigated from a water tank and has a compost system that can get through two kilograms of food waste a day, a vegetable patch and a herb garden.

The choice of cladding was also influenced by the need to not disturb the mature garden. The central part of the house was built in a heavier material — yellow recycled brick selected by the clients as a reminder of both a grandparent's house and their time at Melbourne University. The two pavilion wings use steel cladding, which helped to make the house more lightweight and protected the garden.

Inside, the materials are simple — mostly brick, sustainably sourced timber and concrete. Because concrete is a problematic material, the architects selected a concrete made with fly ash — a by-product of the coal industry — and only used it where it was most helpful for thermal mass. The colour palette is very natural, with the yellow-brown of the bricks tying in nicely with the brown of the timber, especially in the kitchen, which has a hidden pantry and laundry, and the concealed workstation. There are also playful touches, like a net in the children's wing, which creates a fun way to drop down from the top storey to the ground floor below. 'It's about joy and delight,' the architects say. 'We love thinking about everyone in the house, and how they use the house in their ways. And so, we think about what the kids would really enjoy and find the opportunities for creating little moments for them.'

The architects have done everything they can to make this house as sustainable as possible, including using passive design in the orientation of the house, installing insulation in the cavity between double-thickness brick walls and under the floors, and creating high levels of airtightness. Venetian blinds, awnings and fixed shades also manage sunlight penetration.

Garden House is sustainable from head to toe, with environmental considerations built into a range of design decisions. This was in part driven by the clients. Andrew says: 'Instead of [us] saying to clients "Here's this smorgasbord of sustainability potential", [the client said], "It's got to have great air tightness, it's got to have a heat-recovery ventilation system, and of course, it's going to be all electric and fossil-fuel free".' This approach has led to a house that's not only built with the environment in mind, but provides a benchmark in sustainable architecture, while also being a comfortable home for the family who live there.

The children's wing at
the rear is clad in white
metal shingles.

Opposite: The recycled yellow
brick in the main part of
the house evokes memories
for the owners.

Right: The kitchen windows look
onto a small courtyard garden
that is lush with vegetation.

Top: The pool is heated with
highly efficient heat pumps.

Middle: The architects retained
as much of the existing garden
as possible.

Bottom: Built-in bedside tables
are part of the timber joinery.

Opposite: The sitting room
upstairs overlooks the garden.

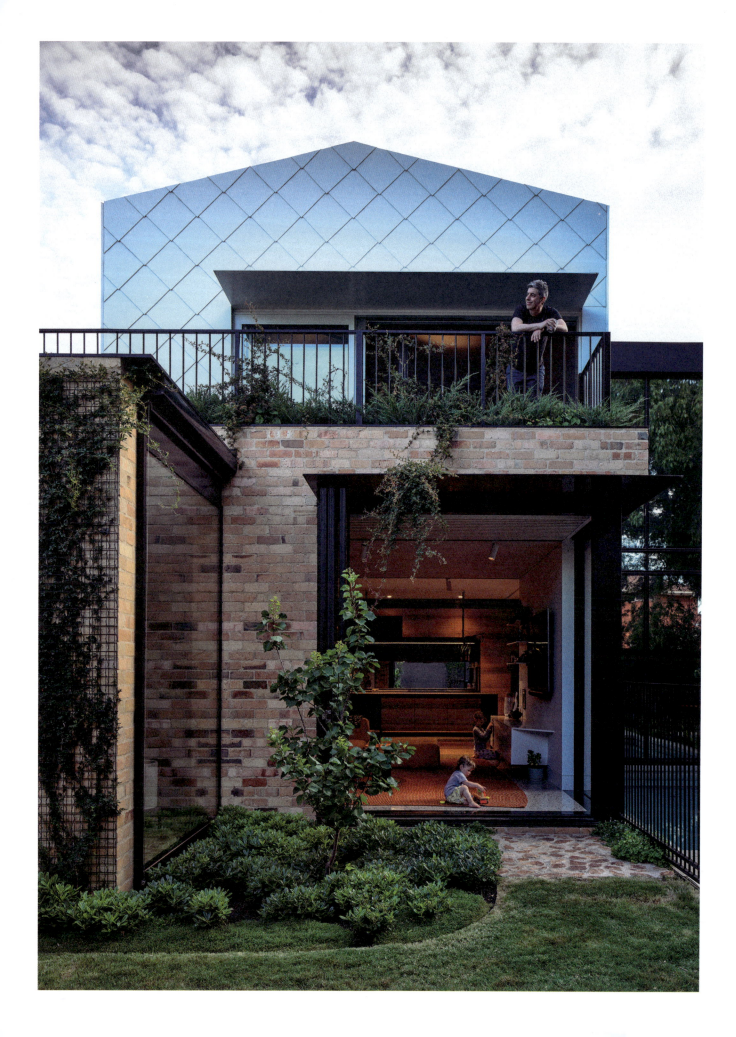

SOLAR AND BATTERIES

When energy from the grid is generated by burning fossil fuels, power generated by solar panels is far preferable. Solar uses the power of the sun to create an electric current, thanks to the photovoltaic effect, which was discovered in 1839. Home solar panels and batteries for storing energy have come into widespread use recently, sparked by rising energy prices and environmental concerns. Using solar panels in a home almost always results in financial savings and increased resale value.

Garden House does not have a gas connection for cooking or heating. It is fossil-fuel free, with the house powered by solar panels that face north, east and west to maximise solar exposure through the day and produce 100 kilowatt-hours of electricity a day. The average Australian home produces 20 kilowatt-hours per day – this house generates five times that. Two batteries store excess electricity, which can be used outside daylight hours or returned to the grid.

Regenerating an ecosystem

PROJECT	Sumu Yakushima, Regenerative Life Studio
LOCATION	Yakushima, Kagoshima Prefecture, Japan
ARCHITECT	tono Inc.
BUILDER	Motchom create
SUSTAINABILITY CONSULTANT	Moss Guide Club/WAKUWORKS
SITE AREA	2548 m²
BUILDING AREA	162 m²
STOREYS	1
PHOTOGRAPHY	Rui Nishi, Hinano Kimoto, Wataru Aoyama

This co-owned home built
off the grid on Yakushima island
was designed to both protect
and regenerate the forest.

SUSTAINABLE FEATURES

Bacteria and mycelium in soil
Battery (50 kW)
Burnt cedar pile foundations
Hemp, charcoal and effective
    microorganism bacteria plaster
Off grid
Radiant-heat cooker
Radiant heating and cooling
    system
River water purified with
    microorganisms and returned
    to nature
Solar (20 kW PV array)

This pavilion house is a regenerative project that preserves and repairs the natural ecology of the World Heritage-listed forests of Japan's Yakushima island, located off the southern coast of Kyushu. Architect Tsukasa Ono is one of eight people who formed the Sumu community, a co-owned retreat on the site of a pair of old cabins that were run as a guesthouse. Tsukasa had visited the cabins, but it wasn't until 2020 that he decided to move here. At the time, the site was managed by Moss Ocean House, which is still responsible for Sumu's programs and building operations.

The cabins have now been replaced with a house made up of six pavilions, but it is so much more than that — nothing less, in fact, than a radical approach to architecture that not only limits damage to the natural environment but actively regenerates it. The word *sumu* means both 'to live' and 'to become clear' — embracing living in a way that has a positive impact on the environment. Fittingly, the first step for Tsukasa and his team was to map the site, learning in depth how water and air flow through the landscape, from the farm at the northern end of the site to the rocky beach and the ocean to the south.

The house has a dining and kitchen pavilion that connects via an outdoor deck to the living room pavilion, and a bathroom pavilion with a freestanding bath. The other three pavilions are bedrooms accessed via winding paths, each with its own deck, two of which are connected. The kitchen is made in local cedar and is designed to encourage social gathering and communication around a large island bench. The layout of the bedroom pavilions vary — one contains built-in bunk beds. 'Sumu is owned by eight private owners, [whose] families are also free to use this facility. The eight of us are very close friends who stay together and spend time together like one family,' explains Tsukasa.

The buildings and decks are raised on stilts, allowing the forest to breathe — water, airflow and forest life is uninterrupted by foundations. In collaboration with experts in the environment, soil and civil engineering, Tsukasa chose a construction method that uses bacteria and mycelium. The carbonised surface of burned wood in the cedar pile foundations promotes the growth of mycelium, encourages tree roots and helps the soil retain water and nutrients. 'This practice has existed since ancient times in Japan. I just translated it into modern times,' explains Tsukasa. 'I was fortunate enough to collaborate with those professionals, and I applied the method to the present day to develop the foundation for Sumu.'

Sumu generates and stores its own solar power and uses local firewood in the wood-fired stoves. Airtightness and insulation also help reduce power costs. The kitchen has a solar-powered radiant heat cooker, and water is drawn from the river basin then purified by microorganisms and returned to nature after use. The primary building material across all the buildings is timber, with a naturally derived persimmon tannin applied near the soil to prevent erosion by insects. Plaster is made from a mix of charcoal and effective microorganisms, providing a healthy, comfortable space that prevents mould and other harmful bacteria. 'Sumu's cottages are built using local cedar wood and are filled with the smell of wood and good air due to the plaster walls issued by good bacteria,' says Tsukasa. A number of ceramic light shades have been made by potters using local clay, meaning the rooms are lit with the colour of the soil.

Tsukasa now lives here for part of the year, when he is not travelling to other cities in Japan and overseas, and the other co-owners and their families visit from time to time as a retreat from the city. 'The room is quiet and very comfortable because it uses radiant air conditioning. Many people who have trouble falling asleep, or who wake up early in the morning, say that they are able to sleep more deeply.'

The concept of regenerative architecture views the buildings we live in as interventions that should not interrupt the natural ecology of the land. When the architects first visited this site, there was a bare camphor tree, an evergreen that had lost its leaves and was dying. As a result of this project, the tree has been revitalised with a thicker trunk and a full canopy of green leaves. For Tsukasa, the deterioration of buildings is a function of nature, and he therefore places importance on the dialogue between nature and architecture.

Below: The dining area is
in one of three pavilions
clustered around a central
timber deck.

Following page: The kitchen
features a solar-powered
radiant-heat cooker and uses
purified water drawn from
the river basin.

Opposite: The living area
has comfortable seating and
a wood-burning fireplace.

Right: The freestanding bath
has expansive views.

REGENERATIVE ARCHITECTURE

Regenerative architecture is an approach to architecture that not only limits harm done to the landscape, but results in a net positive influence on the ecosystem. It requires thorough mapping of the site, including the existing flora and fauna, water and air flows, and the quality of the soil. With a regenerative approach, the environmental and ecological systems surrounding the building will be returned to health.

At Sumu Yakushima, Regenerative Life Studio, the architects took a holistic approach to the entire river basin, from mountains to the sea, considering regenerating the landscape as a vital part of the architecture. They mapped the water and air on site, orienting the building around a healthy flow of the entire basin. They also extended the design of the building underground, using burned wood driven into the earth to promote a mycelial network, and mulch and rice husk charcoal, and cracked and crushed stone, to strengthen the soil.

Opposite: The house's
foundations are burnt cedar
piles, which promote the
growth of mycelium.

Below: The pavilions are
connected by raised timber
decks, leaving enough space
for trees to grow.

House with
a vision

PROJECT	Sheffield House
LOCATION	Sheffield, Massachusetts, USA
ARCHITECT	Of Possible
BUILDER	Kent Hicks Construction Co. Inc.
SUSTAINABILITY CONSULTANT	Energy Efficiency Associates
BUILDING AREA	334 m²
STOREYS	1
PHOTOGRAPHY	Rory Gardiner

Bleached cedar cladding wraps this thermally efficient home whose windows frame cherished family memories.

SUSTAINABLE FEATURES

Airtight construction
Battery (10 kW)
Blown-in mineral wool
  and cellulose
Heat pump (hyperheat)
Heat-recovery ventilation system
Local bluestone
Radiant heating to bathroom floors
Salvaged field stones
Solar (capacity for 5 kW)
Triple-glazed windows

This contemporary minimalist house in the north-east of the USA combines aesthetics with building science. Architect Vincent Appel and his team from Of Possible were tasked with creating a new home on the old family plot. They used high-tech windows and other design and construction techniques to make the home energy efficient.

Located just south of Great Barrington in Massachusetts, Sheffield House replaces the client's childhood home, which was not demolished, but relocated up the hill on a piece of land now owned by the client's sister. The new house fits onto the old foundations and has an efficient floor plan that negated the need for a second storey. The outlook from various rooms frames a series of different locations on the property, including an apple orchard, a small field and an enclave of trees. These are sites of cherished family memories that will form the backdrop for new memories to come. Vincent describes the process of design as 'positioning the house and the program so [the clients] could really live in that experience of the landscape … carrying the memories of the site forward'.

The house is split into two parts — a public zone with a large open-plan kitchen, dining and living room on the southern side of the building that opens onto the deck and garden, and a private zone with bedrooms, bathrooms and a library on the northern side. The two zones can be differentiated by the material underfoot — the polished natural concrete floor in the public zone is specifically detailed and insulated to increase thermal mass, and the white oak floor in the private zone has wide planks that run the full length of each room. The interiors throughout, including the joinery and furnishings, are natural and finished with attention to detail. Vincent says they wanted the project to be 'as calm and as much of a frame for the memories of the site as possible'.

The exteriors are similarly minimal, with bleached cedar siding built to last using continuous length vertical wood boards with enough space behind them for air to circulate. Black flashing joints create horizontal lines around the home, which allow the cedar boards to be laid between them without seams, reducing grime and mineral build-up over time. This subtle detail means the facade will weather evenly. 'Something that looks like a stylised move is performative. It's letting us use material more efficiently,' explains Vincent. 'The way that translates into the actual detailing and architecture … means that that cedar siding is going to be able to breathe and stay dry for easily fifty years.'

With high levels of insulation, air sealing and thermal bridging performance, the home is designed to achieve net zero energy with the addition of a small array of solar panels. The architects worked with the builders to construct the house using some Passive House techniques and systems.

A standing seam metal roof was chosen as a reference to agricultural buildings. It has a one-inch skirt offset and no gutters to create uninterrupted horizontal lines. On the deck, a large-format local bluestone was used for the flooring to complement the concrete floors inside. The walls are highly insulated and overhang the foundation, with the perimeter about half a metre off the yard, creating a seat all the way around the building. 'The entire edge of the building can be used as furniture,' says Vincent. 'Architecturally, the building looks like it floats. This is a fun thing, aesthetically, but it's also functional.'

Initially, the clients were unsure about whether to go contemporary or traditional in the design of the house. They were also unsure if they should keep the existing house or build from scratch. The final approach successfully addressed both these quandaries. The first step was to move, not demolish, the original house. The second was to find a balance in aesthetics without forgetting building performance. The result is a highly sustainable home that combines energy-efficient construction techniques, local materials and material efficiency to create what the architects call a 'marriage of spatial poetry and building science'.

The deck is sheltered under
the roof like an outdoor room.

Top: Polished concrete floors
add to the thermal mass of
the building.

Middle: The floors are polished
concrete in the public zone
and timber in the private zone.

Bottom: The kitchen splashback
is a large window that frames
an established maple tree.

Opposite: Walls overhang the
foundation, creating a sense
that the building is floating.

WINDOWS

The size, type, positioning, orientation and shading of windows, along with their insulating and airtight qualities, have a huge impact on the comfort and energy efficiency of a house. They also determine access to views, nature, light and ventilation, making them crucial to the success of any building.

Sheffield House has Passive House-certified triple-glazed windows with interior wood and exterior aluminium frames. They provide optimal solar heat gain and minimise thermal energy loss. Motorised insect screens are installed on the exterior, allowing windows to be opened completely, and motorised shades can be used in the summer months to block the sun.

Previous page: The living space features a coffee table made from reclaimed oak.

Above: The house creates frames for views.

Opposite: The triple-glazed windows have motorised insect screens and shades.

Energy efficiency with a pinch of salt

PROJECT	Saltbox Passive House
LOCATION	Bromont, Quebec, Canada
ARCHITECT	L'Abri
BUILDER	Rocket Construction
PHIUS CONSULTANT	Sarah Cobb
SITE AREA	10,117 m²
BUILDING AREA	177 m²
FLOOR AREA	288 m²
STOREYS	2
PHOTOGRAPHY	Raphaël Thibodeau

The traditional saltbox shape of this house is combined with the latest in passive design.

SUSTAINABLE FEATURES

Airtight construction
Cellulose insulation
Heat-recovery ventilation system
PHIUS certification
Shou sugi ban
Triple-glazed windows

Francis M Labrecque has always believed that architects have a vital role in addressing the climate crisis. When he co-founded his architecture studio, L'Abri, in Montreal, he and his partners settled on a mantra: people, planet, profit — in that order. This ethos can be seen in their residential projects, including Saltbox Passive House, a house in a small but popular town a couple of hours drive from Montreal that was only the third home in Québec to achieve official Passive House (PHIUS) certification.

The project began when the client visited the second PHIUS-certified house, in Québec's Eastern Townships, and teamed up with the builder from that project to build his own passive house. Francis had recently completed his Passive House training when he came on board. The brief was for a contemporary house that would be the primary residence of a family of four. The client wanted a home that would enable them to enjoy this plot of land, near where he grew up. The house is set on a meadow in an area popular with skiers and has protected views looking down the mountain.

The form of the house is a saltbox — a rural building type that first sprang up in 17th century New England in the USA, and can still be seen there, as well as in this part of Canada. These houses typically have two storeys in the front and one in the back, creating a distinctive sloped roof. Saltbox Passive House follows this basic form. The northern part of the house is built over two storeys and is packed with bedrooms, bathrooms and amenities. The southern part starts with a nearly double-height ceiling and then slopes downwards to a single storey, containing a large open-plan living room, dining room and kitchen. The angle of the roof mirrors the slope of the land, hugging the landscape. The third and lowest level has a garage that is hidden from the other side of the house.

All design decisions were determined by performing an energy model of the building. The house is oriented to promote passive heating of the building, and modelling was used to determine the precise size and location of windows. The house has high levels of insulation, using cellulose for above-ground walls and triple-glazed windows with an airtight envelope, and a heat-recovery ventilation system recovers heat from the air and creates a healthy indoor environment. Francis says, 'It's very simple. Everybody in our climate should use this approach because it makes sense. It's very low tech as well.'

Francis also stresses that the building was a collaboration with the builder and consultants, including a sustainability consultant who is trained in applying Passive House principles. As a result, as well as receiving PHIUS certification, the project also received LEED platinum and PHIUS 2018+ certifications. 'We're doing this for the climate crisis,' says Francis. 'We want to sleep well at night and try to do our part, even though the situation is dire.'

Materials are natural — a timber double-stud structure with wood siding, cellulose insulation, retaining walls made of excavated stone and a roof in grey metal. An entrance section in burnt cedar was inspired by the Japanese technique of *shou sugi ban*. 'We don't want to use too many types of materials,' explains Francis. 'This type of siding has a very good carbon footprint, good durability and is locally sourced.' The interiors also feature simple and sustainable materials. The floor is made of a very thin layer of concrete over timber, instead of a concrete slab, allowing thermal mass while limiting use of this problematic material. 'If we want the construction industry to change, it has to start with the person designing the projects, right?'

Making the most of the traditional saltbox-style housing type, this project shows the success of the Passive House movement in creating energy-efficient homes that are designed specifically for their local climate and have fantastic indoor air quality. It is the first Passive House that L'Abri has completed, but it will not be the last. Energy efficiency has been embedded in the practice since the beginning; the next step is to calculate the carbon footprint of each project. 'Energy efficiency is the easy part and architects get excited about the numbers. But when you start to look at the carbon footprint of what you put in the house, that's a lot of work, and it's as important.'

Previous page: The roof
slants down to one storey
in the dining room.

Opposite: The kitchen cabinets
extend to the second level.

Right: Views of the misty
valley from the upstairs
bedroom.

Top and middle: The stairs connect the one-storey rear with the two-storey section at the front of the house.

Bottom: The kitchen has *shou sugi ban* burnt timber cladding.

Opposite: Materials and colours are simple, with excellent thermal comfort and air quality.

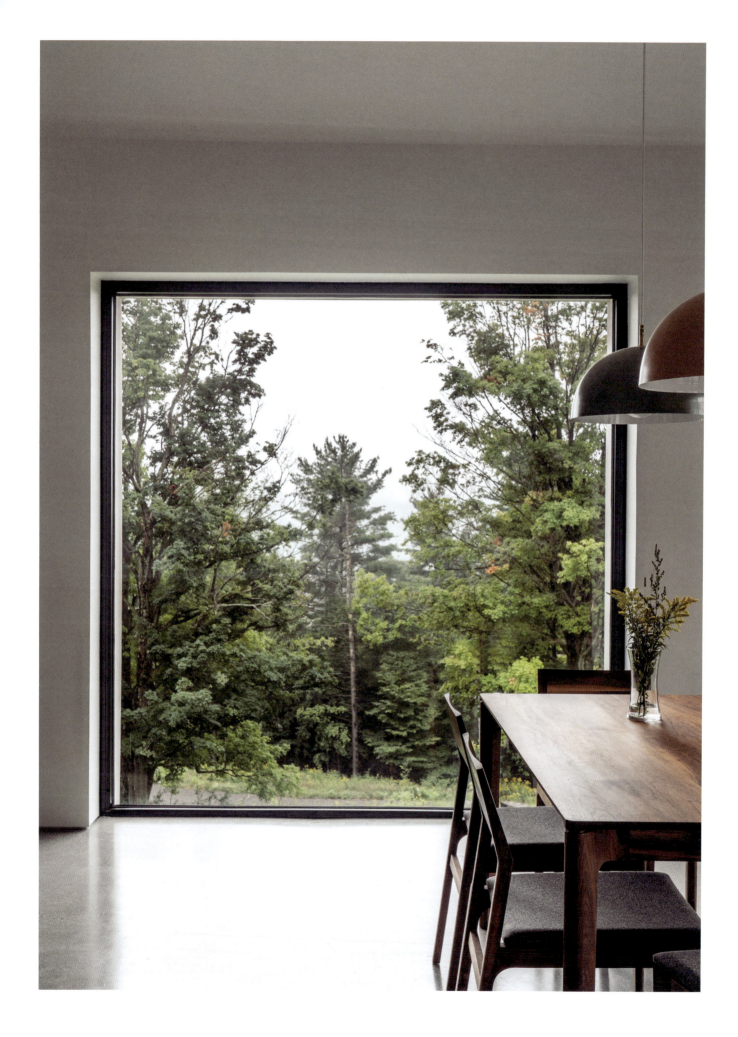

Opposite: A large, insulated window in the dining room frames the trees outside.

Below: The saltbox building includes a basement level where the land falls away.

PASSIVE HOUSE

Passive House is an international design standard that makes use of passive design strategies, such as orientation, window size and placement, and shading, in addition to high levels of insulation and airtightness, heat-recovery ventilation systems and elimination of thermal bridges to achieve high levels of energy efficiency. Originating in Germany, Passive House (or Passivhaus) principles were developed in the 1990s, and Passive House certification is now issued globally.

Saltbox Passive House meets the main principles of Passive House standards:

- a highly insulated and very airtight envelope
- superior heat recovery via a mechanical ventilation system
- a design that optimises the orientation and sizing of openings to promote passive heating of the building.

Saltbox Passive House is only the third house in the Canadian province of Québec to receive PHIUS certification. The architects spent two years documenting the design and construction process of the house and created a web series to help demystify the process for the public.

Prototyping a revolution

PROJECT	HÜTT 01 PassivHaus
LOCATION	Melbourne, Victoria, Australia
ARCHITECT	Melbourne Design Studios
BUILDER	Owner-builder, G-LUX Builders
SUSTAINABILITY CONSULTANT	Melbourne Design Studios, Clare Parry
LANDSCAPE CONSULTANT	Eckersley Garden Architecture
SITE AREA	250 m²
BUILDING AREA	78 m²
FLOOR AREA	178 m²
STOREYS	2 plus attic
PHOTOGRAPHY	Maitreya Chandorkar, Marnie Hawson

Recycled red bricks and garden aquaponics are just two of the sustainable features of this prefabricated passive house.

SUSTAINABLE FEATURES

Battery (6 kW)
Biofuel fireplace
Concrete 70% cement replacement
Cross-laminated timber (CLT)
    structure
Embodied energy reduction
Garden aquaponics with fishpond
    and vertical garden
Green roof
Heat pump
Heat-recovery ventilation system
Passive House Premium
Prefabricated construction

Rain bioretention system
Rainwater tanks
    (3 x 2.56 kL, 4 x 1 kL)
Recycled red brick
Recycled timber deck and beds
Shou sugi ban
Shower heat-recovery unit
Solar (10.6 kW PV array)
Thermal-bridge free airtight
    construction
Triple-glazed windows
Wood-fibre insulation

A pair of German designers has created a prototype for a new kind of housing in Australia with HÜTT 01 PassivHaus. With its distinctive elongated form, black cladding and gabled roof, this prefab house is also their family home. It has achieved the highest possible Passive House certification by using the latest sustainable systems, including a heat-recovery ventilation system, solar power, a heat pump and recycled materials.

When Marc Bernstein-Hussmann and Felicity Bernstein first visited Australia twenty years ago, they realised that Australia had not yet implemented many of the sustainable design solutions that were common in Germany. 'We came here for work and travel, as you do when you are young, and we saw a lot of potential,' says Felicity. The pair moved to Australia and started their practice, Melbourne Design Studios, soon after. They are partners in life and in business — Marc is a registered architect and Felicity is an interior designer. 'The climate is much milder and we thought we'd like to come back and bring our knowledge from Germany and spend some green goodness,' explains Felicity.

Nearly twenty years and many awards later, they found the almost-vacant plot where their new home now stands. Located in an inner-city suburb of Melbourne, it is a cheese-shaped wedge of land that was empty apart from a derelict shed. 'We saw it by pure chance,' says Marc. 'We came across the site, and thought, "What a great opportunity for urban densification on a sustainable level". It's right next to the train line and the bike track.' While the location was perfect, the plot was very small and had limited space at either side. Their solution was to go up. The house is designed as a long two-storey wedge, with two pointed pitched roofs, like witches' hats. The additional storey plus attic space above has allowed Marc and Felicity to fit two living spaces, four bedrooms and three bathrooms on a site with a tiny footprint.

The ground floor has a garage and a courtyard garden at one end and a kitchen and dining space at the other end, with the stairs near the entry and a sunken living room positioned in the centre. Every small space is used. A laundry and bathroom are tucked next to the stairs and a small study is on the right of the entry. On the floor above are four bedrooms and a bathroom, with the main bedroom looking out over a rooftop garden above the garage. The attic space creates a smaller third floor, and contains a landing, a rumpus room, reading nooks and three small bedrooms, each with a black netting beside the beds. It is a great space for kids or adults to hang out.

The home is highly insulated with natural wood-fibre insulation, thermal-bridge-free high-performance windows, a heat-recovery ventilation system and a super-tight building envelope. Heating and cooling are barely ever used, but if needed, are achieved with heat pump technology and a solar panel array and battery. There are three rainwater tanks for toilets, laundry and garden use, plus an extra four for irrigation. The house itself is made with sustainable materials, including recycled bricks, recycled and sustainable timber, an environmentally friendly low-carbon concrete product (with 70 per cent cement replacement) and charred timber cladding.

A green wall and planters cleanse the air indoors, and aquaponics, the green roof and the raingarden are part of a water-sensitive urban design system that keeps more than 90 per cent of stormwater on site. The garden has a fishpond and a vertical garden that is fertilised with fish manure. The run-off from the vertical garden also goes back into the pond. 'In the garden, we also have an aquaponic system, which is really nice. Part of the circular system is a little fishpond that we use as a swimming pond as well in summer. We do jump in and get refreshed,' says Marc.

This is not only a Passive House, it is Passive House Premium, which means it produces more energy than it uses. It has been built using cross-laminated timber, a process that saves unnecessary waste in installation and allows for faster and more accurate construction by prefabricating timber according to the dimensions required — no offcuts go to landfill.

All these sustainable features are the reason that Marc and Felicity plan to replicate this house on other suburban sites around Australia. HÜTT 01 Passive House is a prefabricated Passive House — and number 01 is just the first design. 'We have a number of designs in the drawer, all sketched up and ready to go on typical suburban sites,' says Marc. 'When we set out with the HÜTT idea, the mission was to revolutionise Australia's building industry.' This home is an outstanding example of Passive House design that proves the green revolution is already here.

The architects built vertically
on this small triangular site.

Above: The shower uses
rainwater from onsite tanks,
heated with a heat pump.

Opposite: The kitchen opens out
to the garden, which can be
screened with sheer curtains.

Following page: The sunken
living room looks onto the
small garden wedged between
the main house and the garage.

Top: Every space is used, including an attic with space for reading and sleeping.

Middle: Light filters through the perforated brick exterior onto the staircase.

Bottom: The bathroom features a living green wall and a freestanding bath.

Opposite: The dining space with painting by Richard Dunn and lights by David Trubridge.

Opposite: The interior walls are unfinished prefabricated structural cross-laminated timber panels.

Below: A cosy nook in the attic space has black netting and ladders for safety.

PREFAB

A prefabricated building, or prefab, consists of components that are manufactured elsewhere before being transported and assembled on site. As well as being more affordable and faster to build, prefab architecture has several benefits for the environment, including less materials wastage, a tighter building envelope and less pollution and disturbance of the natural environment.

HÜTT 01 PassivHaus is a prefab design that has been created in several different sizes to fit the dimensions of a typical suburban block. The architects created the prefabricated panels using cross-laminated timber (CLT), an engineered timber with a lower carbon footprint and faster construction time. Internally, the timber also functions as both structure and finish, meaning there is no need to plaster or paint.

Layering with lime

PROJECT	Puigpunyent Eco-Passive House
LOCATION	Puigpunyent, Majorca, Spain
ARCHITECT	Miquel Lacomba Architects
BUILDER	Julio Gracia
SUSTAINABILITY CONSULTANT	José Manuel Busquets Hidalgo (+efficiency)
SITE AREA	400 m²
BUILDING AREA	177 m²
FLOOR AREA	216 m²
STOREYS	2
PHOTOGRAPHY	Mauricio Fuertes

This high-tech passive house
on the island of Majorca has
a traditional Spanish exterior.

SUSTAINABLE FEATURES

Airtight construction
Black cork insulation
Heat-recovery ventilation system
    (double flow)
Lime mortar rendering
Oriented strand board (OSB) panel
    of recycled wood
Recycled cellulose fibre
Recycled steel profiles
Solar (6.16 kW PV array)
Underground water tank (22 kL)
Unfinished internal materials

This house built for an architect and his family in Majorca is an exemplar of sustainable design. Adhering to Passive House principles, the house has sustainable systems, such as solar energy and water tanks, and is made from natural materials, including a natural hydraulic lime mortar on the exteriors and in the roof. The house was designed by Miquel Àngel Lacomba Seguí from Miquel Lacomba Architects on an empty site in Puigpunyent, a little village in the Serra de Tramuntana mountains on the Spanish island of Majorca. The location is a little more remote than other properties he has designed closer to nearby city Palma, but Miquel was confident that the site was right both for him and his family, and for a building that would demonstrate his love of eco-design.

Although Miquel is from Majorca, it was a trip to Sweden in the 1990s that started him on the sustainability path. Back then, sustainability was not practised much and there were few products available for use in this kind of architecture. Scandinavia was ahead of the rest of the world in sustainable design, and also inspired Miquel aesthetically. 'The Scandinavian school impressed me. It's so calm. In the winters, you have to be [inside] and it made you think more slowly and deeply.'

Aesthetically, the exteriors of this home are very Spanish — the roof tiles, slope of the roof and traditional shutters are all regulation in this part of Spain — but the inside shows Miquel's love of Scandinavian design. Using 3D software, Miquel designed built-in shelving for books, storage, sofas, beds, desks and kitchen cupboards made from a single type of fir timber sourced from reforested forests. Many of the pieces have functional details, like the cupboard near the front door, which has built-in lighting, hooks for coats and umbrellas, a bench, a drawer and a shelf at the bottom for shoes. Miquel also designed a fold-out desk in the dining room that can be used by the kids for homework so the family can all be together, then folded away to keep things tidy.

The house is simple in plan, with the garage set to the north of the building and the living areas opening up to the south. At the front, there is privacy to the road, while at the back, the design steps out gradually, due to the slanted boundary line. There are two levels — the living room, kitchen, services, deck and garage are on the ground floor and bedrooms and bathroom are upstairs. Where possible, the house is made with local or natural materials. It has outstanding thermal insulation, control of thermal bridges and airtightness, a heat-recovery ventilation system, photovoltaic solar panels, an underground water tank and a lime mortar rendering on the exteriors.

The walls and roof of the house are layered, with exterior walls made using a highly advanced construction method. The layers consist of natural hydraulic lime mortar rendering, ceramic brick, hydraulic lime mortar rendering, waterproofing sealant with water vapour permeability, fourteen-centimetre expanded black cork insulation and lime-based acrylic finishes. The roof slab is made of timber joists filled with layers of gypsum and recycled cellulose fibre from paper, an airtightness sheet, twenty centimetres of expanded black cork insulation, an oriented strand board panel of recycled wood, a waterproof and breathable vapour-permeable sheet, a four-centimetre layer of lime mortar and Arabic tile on top. These layers result in a highly insulated building envelope that regulates condensation and is resistant to mould. The expanded black cork is particularly interesting — manufactured from the bark of the branches of the cork oak tree, it provides thermal, acoustic and anti-vibration insulation.

Creating high-quality indoor air that is both comfortable and healthy for the family was an important part of the design of the house. 'We talk about a third skin. First we have our skin, then we have our second skin, which is our clothes, then we have our third skin, the house,' explains Miquel. 'I want to avoid materials that have volatile organic compounds. I want healthy quality of air and materials inside because we are the inhabitants.'

This house's stellar sustainable design includes the use of Passive House principles: highly insulated walls and roof, double-glazed windows, control of thermal bridges, good airtightness, a heat-recovery ventilation system, solar and water tanks, and mainly local materials and construction processes. But it is also a highly liveable home designed first and foremost for family. Miquel describes it as a generous, open-hearted place for gatherings, for music and drawing, and for happy moments.

Cabinets in the dining room
fold out to become a desk.

Top: The exterior walls and roof are layered with lime mortar.

Middle: This built-in cupboard for coats, shoes and hats near the front door includes integrated lighting.

Bottom: Much of the furniture, including this bedhead, is made from fir timber.

Opposite: The kitchen, like the rest of the house, is simple white and timber.

LIME MORTAR

Lime mortar is a low-carbon material — it emits less carbon during its manufacture and actually absorbs carbon from the atmosphere after hardening. Hydraulic lime mortar sets by hydrolysis, a reaction caused by water that is faster and harder than non-hydraulic lime. Lime mortar is also a natural material that will not cause damage to, or pollute, air, water or soil. And at the end of its life, lime mortar is completely recyclable.

Hydraulic lime mortar was used in layers on the exterior walls and in the roof of Puigpunyent Eco-Passive House. It was chosen for its ability to regulate humidity in a natural way — lime is hydroscopic, which means it draws the moisture from the internal environment to the exterior, helping to control condensation and stop the growth of mould.

Previous page: The architect designed the Scandi-inspired blonde timber interiors.

Above: Family gatherings on the deck make this house meaningful.

Opposite: Lime mortar is insulating and also regulates humidity naturally.

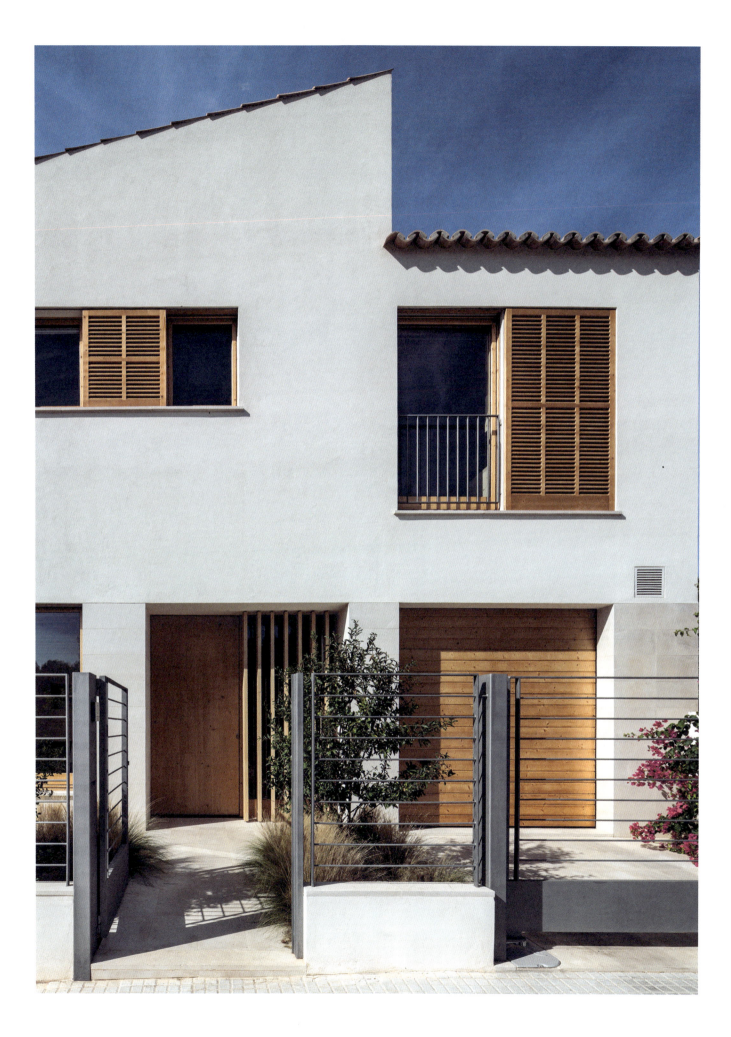

Living lightly in the forest

PROJECT	Anawhata House
LOCATION	Anawhata, West Auckland, New Zealand
ARCHITECT	Paul Davidson
BUILDER	Simon Spierer and Paul Davidson
SITE AREA	2 ha
BUILDING AREA	68 m²
FLOOR AREA	118 m²
STOREYS	2
PHOTOGRAPHY	Simon Wilson

Built with a deliberately
small footprint, this house
has an ecologically friendly
construction.

SUSTAINABLE FEATURES

Foundations drilled to avoid
    tree roots
Reclaimed black maire timber
Shou sugi ban
Timber water tank with
    potable-grade liner
Wastewater system
Wood burner with wetback
    water heater

Having already renovated a bungalow in Dunedin in the south of New Zealand with his partner before relocating to Auckland to retrain as an architect, Paul Davidson decided the time was right to buy an empty plot of land and build their own home. To do the least amount of damage to the environment, the home was designed with systems such as water tanks, an onsite wastewater treatment system and a wood-burning stove. It also has a deliberately small footprint, with foundations drilled into the forest floor so as not to upset tree roots.

The first step of the project was to choose a site. The couple chose a spot with a gentle slope and a north-facing aspect to capture winter sun on a 5-acre block in the forests of Anawhata, less than an hour's drive from Auckland. Paul used his previous experience as an industrial designer, combined with his new training in architecture, to complete the project. 'I came from industrial design so designing the outside of the building was something that came naturally to me,' says Paul. 'But planning spaces is a very different aspect of design. I resolved the planning with the help of my lecturers.'

The key to the planning, it turned out, was bringing the entry and stairs to the centre of the plan. The entry to the house is from a raised deck at the side, which can also be used for dining during the warmer months. From the small entry space, there is a bedroom to the left and an open-plan kitchen and living room to the right. Upstairs are two smaller rooms: a TV annexe on one side, and a second bedroom, now the baby's room, on the other.

The exteriors are determined by the interior plan — the main bedroom is clad in semi-translucent polycarbonate, which keeps this room private but also creates a paper lantern effect, like a Japanese shoji screen, especially when lit up at night. This material also has less heat loss than glass.

The more public end of the house, where the kitchen and living room are, has large sliding glass doors with views of the surrounding forest. The interiors are clad in plywood, which Paul installed himself. Reclaimed black maire timber — native to New Zealand and incredibly hardwearing — was used for the floorboards and kitchen benchtops. 'It's a native timber — logs that were cut down a long time ago to make farmland and were just left to rot. Timber merchants have been pulling out these logs and reclaiming the timber.'

Originally cleared before World War II, but not built on, the clearing where the house now stands had trees that were about eighty years old. The house was constructed so it did not impinge on the natural environment. Building the house in two storeys was a way of keeping the footprint of the house small. Even the foundations were made by drilling in exposed piles and bearers rather than pouring a slab, so as not to disturb tree roots. 'The drilling of piles allows you to move this way or that if need be,' explains Paul. 'If you realise that there's a big root here, then you just move to the left or the right and leave the root there.'

As well as its sustainable materials and ecologically friendly construction, the house has a number of sustainable systems, such as a timber water tank that collects water off the roof with a potable grade liner. It also has a recirculating textile filter system that treats water and then disperses it over a large area via driplines to allow the water to be absorbed back into the forest floor. The house is heated by a wood-burning stove that also has a wetback that heats the water. Due to the climate, the house doesn't need cooling in summer, just cross-ventilation.

For Paul and his small family, living here has been a positive experience. 'We've had some big storms out here and it just feels so safe and secure. We sit beneath the roof and listen to this really heavy rain and it's just a joy. It's shelter, but it's also really a delight to live in.'

For Paul, architecture is about combining three things: art, function and science. The art is about making you 'feel something when you are inside a building' and the function is 'the human aspect, anthropometrics and ergonomics, the shelter aspect, whether the materials stand up to the climate,' explains Paul. And the science element is sustainability. 'Trying to reduce our emissions long term and trying to reduce our carbon footprint. It has to answer all the other questions, last a long time and not make the planet worse.'

The wood-burning stove
in the living room doubles
as a water heater.

Opposite: Above the timber
kitchen is a TV annexe and
the baby's room.

Right: Wastewater from the
house is collected in a timber
water tank, treated and
returned to nature.

Following page: Reclaimed
black maire timber was used
as flooring and the walls are
plywood.

Opposite: Firewood is stored under the step to the deck.

Below: The bedroom wall is a translucent screen that is more insulating than glass but also lets light through.

PILE FOUNDATIONS

A house's foundations can have a huge impact on soil, groundwater, noise, vibration and carbon emissions. Concrete slabs may have a high thermal mass but are also one of the largest contributors to embodied carbon and practically impossible to recycle. If the aim is to do as little damage to the environment as possible, drilling vertical piles directly into the earth is one of the best solutions.

At Anawhata House, the quantity and proximity of trees, many of which are old, meant that foundations would disrupt tree roots. The solution was to drill vertically, so that each pile could be moved if necessary. The building was elevated with a suspended floor to keep it dry and avoid the need for deeper excavations for drainage. In heavy rain, the entire hillside can turn into a sheet of water, so being up above the ground makes a lot of sense. Being up higher also means more sun.

Wrapped in a protective skin

PROJECT	Camp O
LOCATION	Catskill Mountains, New York, USA
ARCHITECT	Maria Milans Studio
SUSTAINABILITY CONSULTANT	I + I Studio
SITE AREA	6 ha
BUILDING AREA	123 m²
FLOOR AREA	195 m²
STOREYS	2 plus basement
PHOTOGRAPHY	Montse Zamorano

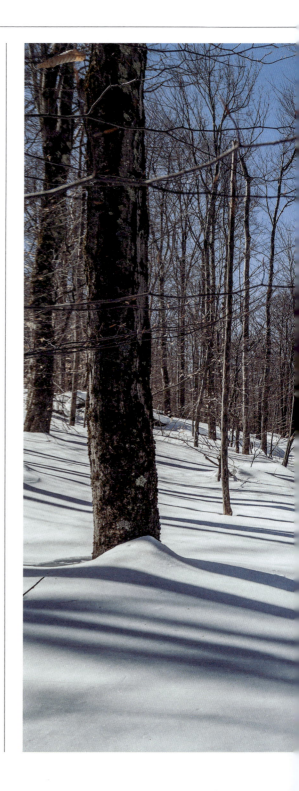

The house has a split roof, angled up at one end and down at the other, and highly insulated exterior walls.

SUSTAINABLE FEATURES

Exterior insulation
Fireplace
Radiant underfloor heating
Shou sugi ban
Thermal-bridge free
Unfinished internal materials
Wood-fibre panel

This combined house and studio has a small footprint, a clever sloping roof and a novel approach to construction that minimises its energy consumption, despite the dramatic temperature swings of its location.

Maria Milans from Maria Milans Studio and her husband bought an empty plot of land to build their own home to live and work in — before COVID-19 lockdowns made working from home compulsory. They chose a remote site in the Catskill Mountains, south-east of New York City, USA. They are surrounded by state forests and their closest neighbour is 800 metres away, but they are only a two-and-a-half-hour drive from New York City. The previous owner had made a clearing, using the timber for firewood, but had never got around to building. Using this already cleared land reduced the environmental impact of the building considerably.

Maria realised that there were two aspects the building's design had to take advantage of — the amazing outlook down the mountain to the west, and the morning sun that streams in from the east. As a result, the house is split into two. The smaller, front part of the house is dense with bedrooms, bathrooms and amenities and features a master bedroom with views of the mountain. The back of the house is much more open, with a double-height void above a large open-plan kitchen, dining and living room, and a work space on the mezzanine balcony that captures the morning sun and has treetop vistas.

This layout allowed the house to be compact, yet expansive where it needed to be. At ground level, the main living space opens onto a deck that is sheltered by the overhang of the second storey above. Unlike many houses in the area, which either have a basement or are perched above the ground, this house has a concrete slab and a U-shaped retaining wall, with a space that opens directly onto the deck and garden at the same level, creating a sense of connection between the indoors and the outdoors. 'Half of the foundation of the house was a retaining wall, but the other half was open to the view,' explains Maria. 'We decided that that was going to be the main living area and that we could go out directly onto the garden.'

On the exterior, charred timber, inspired by the Japanese technique of *shou sugi ban*, has been used to create a robust cladding that looks great in the forest setting. The main structure of the house is parallel strand lumber and Douglas fir plywood. These materials are common in the local area, and were chosen because the contractors would be familiar with them, but the method of construction was changed. This timber is usually covered with plaster or gypsum, with insulation in-between, and a number of joists to connect the gypsum that unfortunately create thermal bridges. 'Normally, you have thermal bridges every time you have a stud. I wanted to avoid that, I wanted to do something way more efficient,' says Maria.

The solution was to leave the timber as is, and attach a layer of solid insulation on the outside of the house, along with a charred-timber rainscreen, to create a continuous insulated surface around the exterior and minimise thermal lag. This exterior wall construction system follows a pressure-equalised rainscreen insulated structure technique (PERSIST) that creates an extremely well insulated home. As a result, the interiors show the exposed structural timber. 'You don't normally get to see that timber because it's all covered with insulation and plaster,' says Maria. 'I felt that showing the structure is beautiful.'

While timber is the main material used in the construction of the house, concrete was used to build the floor and walls that are in direct contact with the ground, and a composite made of cement and wood fibre was used on the second-storey floor and all surfaces in the bathrooms and kitchen, because it has good thermal lag and is water resistant.

The intense temperature swings in the Catskills, not just between summer and winter, but between day and night, as well as intense winds and sun meant that energy efficiency was key. As well as maximising the winter sun, shielding the western sun and providing cross-ventilation with facades to protect the home from strong winds, the architects installed a radiant underfloor heating system supplemented by a fireplace on the coldest side of the house.

Architecture is a response to place — the weathering of seasons and temperature, site conditions and materials. This home and studio in the Catskills offers a solution to the local surroundings that also prioritises energy efficiency and creates a comfortable living space. 'Great architecture is aiming for efficiency and to live in a better environment,' says Maria. 'I think nowadays we should not only think about how the building looks but how it interacts with its environment.'

Below: The rear of the house
has a double-height ceiling and
a mezzanine studio.

Following page: The structural
timber is completely exposed.

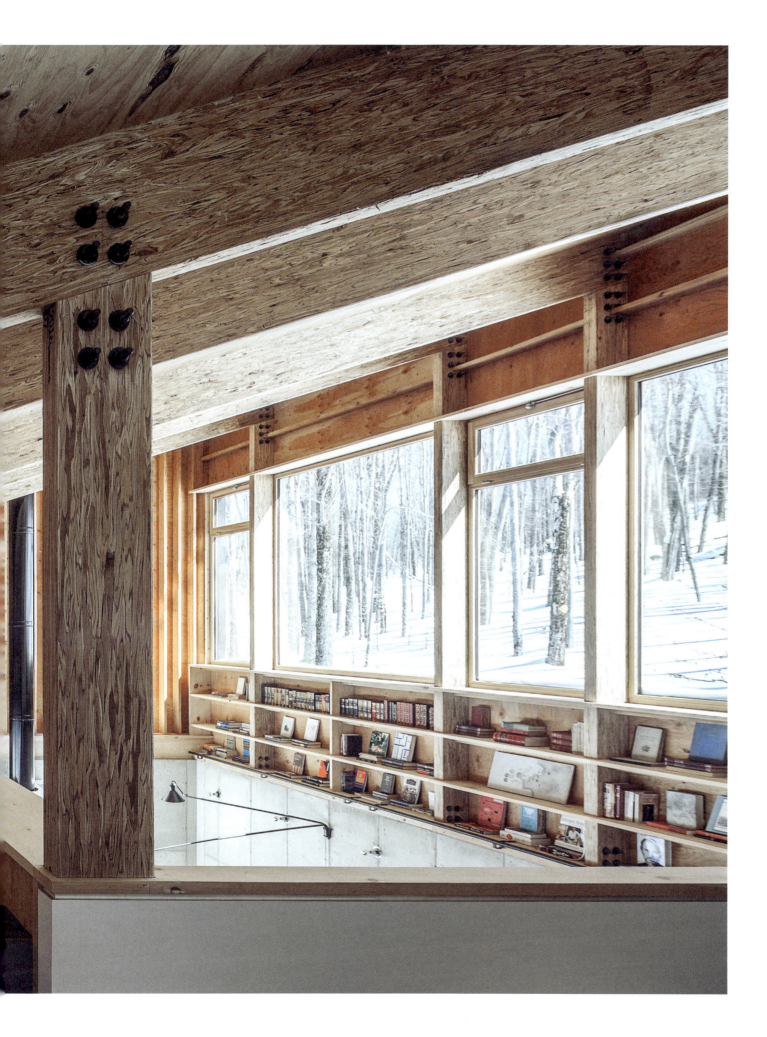

Top: The view from the master
bedroom looks across the
staircase void to the mountains
beyond.

Middle: The living room opens
to the deck and garden.

Bottom: Raised bookshelves
in the main living space are
accessible by ladder.

Opposite: The floor and walls
in contact with the ground are
concrete, with timber above.

EXTERIOR INSULATION

Although attaching insulation to the exterior of buildings is often used as an easy way to retrofit old properties, this can also be done on new buildings, with untreated structural timber used in the interior finish of a house and all functional insulation and waterproofing on the exterior.

At Camp O, the architects left the timber structure and siding on the inside of the house unfinished and constructed an insulated wall system, which also acts as a rainscreen, on the exterior. This system follows a pressure-equalised rainscreen insulated structure technique (PERSIST) that was developed in Canada by the National Research Council to maximise effectiveness and durability. The wall system balances interior and exterior air pressure with an air/vapour barrier, creating a continuous watertight and insulated envelope that minimises thermal bridges and achieves good thermal lag.

Above: View from the mezzanine studio down the staircase to the level below.

Opposite: The exterior skin is structural and highly insulated and also acts as a rainscreen.

Many hands
make hempcrete

PROJECT	Hempcrete House
LOCATION	Lyonville, Victoria, Australia
ARCHITECT	Altereco Design
BUILDER	Sarah Corbet (owner-builder)
SUSTAINABILITY CONSULTANT	Northern Environmental Design
SITE AREA	3 ha
BUILDING AREA	77 m²
FLOOR AREA	106 m²
STOREYS	2
PHOTOGRAPHY	Jade Cantwell

This compact home is made
of hempcrete poured by the
owner-builders and volunteers.

SUSTAINABLE FEATURES

Airtight construction
Clay plaster and clay paint
Clean-burning wood heater
Double-glazed windows
Earth wool insulation
Fire rating BAL-29
Heat pump (315 L tank)

Hempcrete walls with lime render
Plywood reused from
   hempcrete formwork
Reclaimed messmate timber
Reclaimed spotted gum
Recycled glass benchtops
Solar (6.5 kW PV array)
Water tanks (50 kL, 60 kL, 22 kL)
Worm septic system

When it comes to renewable, biodegradable building materials, hempcrete has many advantages. It is a non-toxic building material that has the same thermal mass benefits of concrete but is made from plant material. It is fireproof (an important consideration in many parts of the world), regulates humidity naturally and is resistant to pests, rot and mould. It is also carbon negative, meaning that it will absorb carbon from the atmosphere for the life of the building. That's why, despite the slow uptake of hempcrete by the construction industry, owners Sarah Corbet and David Bruce chose to use it for their new home.

The project began when Sarah and David bought an empty, disused 3-hectare farm plot in the small regional hamlet of Lyonville, north of Melbourne. Their brief to architecture studio Altereco Design was for a house that they could eventually retire to, but the first step was to build a shed that they could live in while they built the house. Sarah and David were not just owner-builders, they were also physically involved in the building process, including pouring the hempcrete themselves with the help of volunteers.

The other part of the brief was to create a house that had a small footprint. The simple, compact floorplan reflects this, with living and dining spaces, a kitchen and a bathroom downstairs, and a bedroom with a built-in desk on the mezzanine level above. The roof slopes steeply upwards to accommodate the mezzanine — the main bedroom, and the living spaces directly below, are oriented towards the best views to the east of the dam and the forest, and the living room also catches the northern sun. 'They wanted to live pretty lightly on the land. That was the key motivation to the building they created,' explains architect James Goodlet. 'I don't recall designing something before that felt so spacious, but that we knew was actually quite small. They were conscious of their literal footprint, but are also very conscious of their environmental impact as well.'

Choosing hempcrete was a way of addressing this environmental impact. The hempcrete was poured on site into a temporary formwork that was built around the timber frame of the house and removed after about two hours, when the hempcrete had set. '[When] the timber frame for the house is complete and erected, you're literally building the formwork and then moving up in layers as it cures,' explains James.

This building method is labour-intensive but achievable for owner-builders. The wet hempcrete mix is transferred with buckets into the formwork and manually compressed around the edges. Sarah and David did a call out on social media for volunteers and people came from across the state to help and learn about hempcrete. 'We wanted to build something that showcased a high-performing sustainable home that was climate resilient,' explain Sarah and David.

Using hempcrete also helped to make the house resistant to fire, along with fire-resistant paint on the external timber elements, achieving Bushfire Attack Level BAL-29. As well as hempcrete, other sustainable materials used in the home include internal stud walls lined with the plywood reused from the hempcrete formwork; reclaimed messmate for the front door, staircase, banister and kitchen cupboard fronts; recycled glass benchtops; and earth wool insulation. David also made the internal timber doors, skirting boards, architraves and shelves from recycled messmate floorboards. Outside, reclaimed spotted gum was used on the posts, cladding and eave linings. The house also has a hot water heat pump, a solar photovoltaic system, several rainwater tanks, non-gas appliances and a worm-based septic system.

The resulting home feels warm, spacious and tranquil and has a sense of being in nature — an expansiveness. The house is oriented north for winter sun, has a fully insulated concrete slab for thermal mass, casement windows for good ventilation, large ceiling fans and skylights that act as hot air vents in winter. 'Living in the house is amazing,' say Sarah and David. 'We rarely use any heating. In winter, it can be zero degrees outside and maintain an inside temperature of nineteen to twenty-two degrees without heating.'

Below: The living room is bright and quiet — hempcrete is an excellent acoustic insulator.

Following page: The large kitchen features recycled timber and a walk-in pantry.

Top: The staircase and banister are made of recycled messmate timber.

Middle: The house has a heat pump for hot water and a worm septic system.

Bottom: The clean-burning wood heater is only used in extended cold and frosty weather.

Opposite: The concrete slab has good thermal mass and the windows are double glazed.

HEMPCRETE

Hemp is a versatile crop that restores soil fertility, fixes nitrogen in the soil and uses less water than crops such as cotton. The seeds and flowers can be used in medicines, and the fibres and stalks in clothing and paper. Hempcrete is made from hemp shives or hurd — the inner woody part of the fibre — combined with lime binder and water. It has excellent insulating and acoustic properties; is resistant to pests, rot and mould; is fireproof; and absorbs and stores carbon dioxide from the atmosphere.

The owner-builders of Hempcrete House chose hempcrete for its thermal efficiency and comfort, wanting a healthy breathable house that regulates its own humidity, and also has thermal mass and fire resistance. They poured the hempcrete themselves with the help of volunteers. A plywood formwork was created and the 300 mm hempcrete walls were poured in layers, with each layer setting before the next was poured.

Opposite: The front entry
features both finished and
unfinished hempcrete walls.

Below: Upstairs, the
unfinished hempcrete creates
an unusual texture above
the built-in desk.

A down-to-earth city pad

PROJECT	Karper
LOCATION	Molenbeek, Brussels, Belgium
ARCHITECT	Hé! Architectuur
BUILDER	Het Leemniscaat
SUSTAINABILITY CONSULTANT	EA+
SITE AREA	200 m²
BUILDING AREA	2021 m²
FLOOR AREA	128 m² (64 m² per floor)
STOREYS	2 (apartment only)
PHOTOGRAPHY	Tim Van de Velde

Part of the adaptive reuse
of an abandoned building,
this home features a range
of flexible spaces and
innovative materials.

SUSTAINABLE FEATURES

Designed for disassembly
Prefabricated wooden cassettes
Recycled radiators
Straw bale insulation
Waste soil used for plaster
   and rammed earth

This home in Brussels, Belgium, achieves a number of different sustainable objectives: urban renewal and the adaptive reuse of an abandoned building, a co-owned multipurpose building with several tenants, a novel approach to materials (including the use of straw in the walls and recycled urban earth) and finally, an eye to the future and the disassembly of materials for reuse.

Hanne Eckelmans from Hé! Architectuur designed and renovated this project, which includes her own apartment. The story begins when Hanne's friends found a dilapidated building in the inner-city Brussels suburb of Molenbeek, which has an industrial past and a thriving Moroccan community. It was not liveable — all the windows were broken and Hanne says it was 'raining inside'. The building was made up of two parts connected by an internal courtyard — the back had been an industrial building where disinfectant was made, and the front was previously offices. Hanne's friends were keen on the back, while Hanne and her then-boyfriend saw potential in the front, so the two couples bought the building together.

To achieve their vision, a permit had to be obtained, not just to build but also to change the function of the property to mixed use so that both couples could live in it and also rent sections to other businesses and residents. The other opportunity that the front part of the building provided was to build an extra two storeys — luckily the buildings on either side were already at this height, so it was not difficult to get permission. 'I saw immediately the possibility to build something on top,' says Hanne. 'It's lower than the two neighbours and I thought "This is cool, to do new construction on top of an old house".'

Now, after a complete transformation of both buildings, Hanne lives in a two-storey apartment in the front building and has a private roof terrace on the level above. Her main living spaces are on the second floor of the building, and the kitchen and dining space are on the third floor, along with a void that overlooks the level below. The first floor contains a separate studio apartment that is currently rented, although this may change in future. 'The idea was that it's flexible and that the three levels could eventually combine into one family house, with the bedrooms more at level one, and the living spaces at two and three,' explains Hanne. The front building also houses a co-working space on the ground floor and the underground level below. The back half of the project (not designed by Hanne) now includes an apartment for the co-owners of the property, as well as a mix of additional residential and commercial spaces.

The materials chosen for this project are innovative — biobased, geobased, biodegradable, renewable and recycled. The existing facades are insulated with hemp lime blocks and many of the interior finishes are made with a local lime plaster similar to a Moroccan *tadelakt* lime plaster. Other interior finishes include plaster made from a mixture of sand and clay that was recycled from earthmoving projects, and rammed earth. This aspect of the project was led by Hanne's boyfriend at the time, Nicolas Coeckelberghs, a partner at BC Materials. Hanne says, 'They transform waste earth from digging a new metro line into building materials, such as the earth plaster that we used for the walls and rammed-earth kitchen islands.'

The outer shell of the new roof was constructed from prefabricated wood filled with straw bales from a local farm, which raised eyebrows from the neighbours when they were delivered. 'The straw bales are not so common in the inner urban area and all our neighbours were super surprised,' says Hanne. 'We rented little lifts to pull them all up and the neighbours saw that we were bringing lot of straw into the house and they didn't understand. "What are you doing there? Do you have chickens up there?".'

The new parts of the building were clad in brick, to complement the existing red brick of the ground floor and surroundings. Recycled, second-hand materials include radiators from Hanne's grandmother's house, which was being renovated at the time. The structure was left visible in many places in order to make it possible to see any problems and fix them down the line, or swap them out and recycle them. 'Eventually you can easily disassemble your building after many years if you need to,' explains Hanne. Every element of this project has been thought through with a community-minded and circular mindset, acknowledging the role of design, not just for now, but for the future.

The architect now lives in
the two new storeys at the
front of the original building.

Top: The terraces are stepped
from one level to the next.

Middle: The studio on the level
below is currently tenanted.

Bottom: Finishes on the walls
include lime plaster and a
plaster made from waste earth.

Opposite: The open-plan living
space can be divided with sheer
curtains.

Previous page: The level change between the terrace and the bathroom creates the effect of a sunken bath.

Opposite: The kitchen features a rammed earth island.

Below: The waste earth used in the island was sourced from a construction site.

WASTE EARTH MATERIALS

Rammed earth is a construction method that involves compacting soil mixtures into walls or columns. It is non-toxic, non-polluting and breathable, has excellent thermal mass, and is low in embodied energy. Using waste soil from earthmoving construction projects, such as foundations for new buildings or tunnels, is even more environmentally friendly.

For Karper, a kitchen island was constructed from three rammed-earth blocks made with recycled waste geomaterials. A recycled earth wall plaster was also made with a mixture of sand and clay. The plaster creates a healthy indoor environment, is vapour-permeable, regulates humidity and has superior acoustic and insulating properties. A workshop was also held to train five local contractors in how to apply earth plasters.

On the coast and off the grid

PROJECT	Bass Coast Farmhouse
LOCATION	Bass Coast, Victoria, Australia
ARCHITECT	Wardle
BUILDER	Overend Constructions
SUSTAINABILITY CONSULTANT	greensphere
SITE AREA	66 ha
BUILDING AREA	375 m²
STOREYS	2
PHOTOGRAPHY	Trevor Mein

The house appears to
balance lightly on the
ridge of the hill.

SUSTAINABLE FEATURES

Battery (185 kW)
Heat pump
Hydronic floor heating
Off grid
Onsite wastewater treatment
Prefabricated steel framing,
    stud walls and lining
Recycled spotted gum floorboards
Solar (31 kW PV array)
Water tanks (2 x 1 kL)

This new house in a remote area on the south coast of Victoria was built to withstand unhospitable weather, which can include winds of up to 190 kilometres per hour. It has an internal courtyard and shutters that can be closed completely or opened up. A large house on a remote site, it is designed to be sustainable with off-grid electricity and water tanks large enough to tackle bushfires as well as day-to-day watering needs.

Designed by John Wardle, this is the third house his architecture practice, Wardle, has created for the same clients. The first was an apartment in the city, the second was a beach house and this one was envisioned as the quintessential country house. The brief was for a home that would be comfortable for a family of three and could also be used to host large groups.

The house sits on a large block of land about two-and-a-half hours' drive from Melbourne. Where on the site to build was the first question — rather than building close to the ocean, the architects proposed that the house be set back slightly, offering views of the landscape and the sea beyond.

From afar, the house looks almost cartoonish in its simplicity. It has a timber exterior, galvanised iron roof and chimney, and only three types of windows across the whole building. Inside, the complexity of the architecture becomes apparent. Firstly, this is a courtyard house. The outdoor space at the centre is sheltered from the high winds. Shutters allow the house to be completely shut down for protection or opened up if the weather is nice. Secondly, the house is not on a flat piece of land. Parts of the house seem to float over the ground in what John calls 'structural gymnastics'. He says, 'The gabled roof structure and the walls are constant, but the house pirouettes across the rise in a two-way cantilever, reaching out from two directions across the fall in the landscape.'

The structure is anchored by two concrete slabs on two levels, while timber is the overriding material used across the project. Recycled spotted gum is used for the floors, hardwood for the window frames and external cladding, and a veneer lines the rest of the interiors. The result is a home that feels warm and natural, that can glow on sunny days or be quite moody on dark days. John is known for his proclivity for timber, but has moved away from always using solid timber. 'Using veneers is a very efficient way of employing timber for a lining material,' he says. 'And recycled where we can on the flooring.'

There is a calmness that comes from the symmetry of the house. Two of the four sides are exact mirror images of the other, each one containing a double bedroom, a bathroom and a bunk room. Other families can come to visit, but they each have a side of the house to themselves. 'I think there's a feeling of calm when you think of courtyards,' says John. 'Like Buddhist monasteries and Japanese Shinto religious structures, where the courtyard itself is a place of contemplation. The house creates that contemplative experience.'

Solar orientation has been used to minimise heating and cooling, and the shutters allow the owners to control the sun and wind according to the time of day or seasons of the year. The house also has a high degree of sealed insulation in floors, walls and ceilings. The steel framing, stud walls and lining section were made in Melbourne to minimise material wastage on site. The house is off grid, with solar and battery storage at a distance from the house that supplies all onsite electricity. Rainwater is harvested from the roof and stored in the shed, and two large water tanks provide enough water for the house, garden and swimming pool and have nozzles for firefighting. The house also has a heat pump and hydronic floor heating system and a septic system that manages all wastewater on site, used for landscaping.

These sustainable systems and materials combine to create a house that follows the maxim to do as little harm to the environment as possible. John says, 'We have to look carefully at the responsibility of building. Building itself is almost a wilful act. And we have to make sure that if we are to build, we're absolutely minimising our impact as much as possible.'

Below: Spotted gum veneer walls and ceilings change with the light.

Following page: Based on a farmhouse, the simple plan has a central kitchen and dining area.

Top: Each shutter is operated by a handheld wheel.

Middle: Bedrooms and bathrooms are on either side of the main space.

Bottom: Open shelving in the kitchen, with view down one side of the hall.

Opposite: The house sits on a large block of land and has views of the surrounding landscape.

OFF GRID

Going off grid means not having to rely on a connection to standard utilities and infrastructure such as electricity, gas, water and sewerage. One of the environmental benefits of going off grid is not using fossil fuels, as solar energy offers a much cleaner, more renewable option. Using your own water system also contributes to water conservation. Having your own solar power, water and wastewater treatment can also be more reliable and save you money.

At Bass Coast Farmhouse, a 31-kilowatt solar PV array feeds into a huge 185-kilowatt battery located in a nearby shed. Two 10,000-litre water tanks store rainwater harvested from the roof, providing drinking water and supplying the swimming pool. It is also used in the underfloor hydronic heating system and the water tanks can be fitted with firehose nozzles for fighting fires.

Opposite: The lower ground
level has a cellar, laundry,
outdoor kitchen and terrace.

Below: Shutters protect the
house from inclement weather
and can be opened for views
and light.

Building better with bamboo

PROJECT	Echo House
LOCATION	Green Village, Bali, Indonesia
ARCHITECT	IBUKU
BUILDER	PT Bamboo Pure
SITE AREA	963 m²
BUILDING AREA	302 m²
FLOOR AREA	395 m²
STOREYS	2
PHOTOGRAPHY	Tommaso Riva, Indra Wiras

This house is one of a number
of buildings at Green Village
made using advanced bamboo
construction techniques.

SUSTAINABLE FEATURES

Bamboo construction
Groundwater tank

Echo House is one of eighteen unique bamboo houses by design studio IBUKU at Green Village, located on the Ayung River Valley in Bali. Designed for the tropical climate and nestled among the trees, the house demonstrates the superior qualities of bamboo as a functional, flexible and uniquely sustainable construction material.

IBUKU is a multidisciplinary design studio based in Bali and run by Elora Hardy that has become known for its bamboo constructions. The studio's roots go back to the 1990s, when Elora's father, John Hardy, first started designing and building structures made from bamboo. Elora took over the business in 2010 and now employs a diverse team of architects, engineers and local craftspeople. To date, IBUKU has built over 200 structures, including houses, restaurants, hotels and more. 'I haven't trained as an architect,' says Elora. 'Normal architectural processes are not applicable because of the nature of the material... On one hand, it's been challenging, creating buildings without having been trained. And on the other hand, I've been told it can be an asset, because if I knew, I never would have been crazy enough to do this.'

Echo House is one of IBUKU's most recent private houses in Green Village, built for an international German–Australian family. The site is on a slope above a river, and the house is nestled into the incline, surrounded by black palm and coconut trees. The main part of the house, which has a separate kids' living space and a main living room, is in the centre of the site; two smaller bedroom wings are on either side, and there is a poolside kitchen on the ground floor.

Bamboo is used not just for the external walls , floors, ceilings, screens, window frames and balustrades, but also for furniture, light shades and structures like the support that holds a strip light in the children's space. Even the kitchen and bathroom have bamboo walls. 'We have to find how it can be cohesive, because it's so far outside of the normal conversation. Suddenly you put a light switch on a wall and it stands out in a way it wouldn't on a conventional wall because you're in a different story,' says Elora. Alongside the bamboo, the roof is made of copper shingles, the ground is local stone, and the house features steel, glass, terrazzo, wood and local brick.

Bamboo is the material of choice for many of IBUKU's Bali projects, because of its incredible versatility. As well as providing a strong base for buildings, it can be used for many exterior and interior finishes as well as fittings. Echo House has benefitted not only from the use of bamboo, but from the innovative construction techniques that IBUKU has developed, such as curved bamboo. 'We had to gather a team together and come up with all these construction methods. Craftsmen have a long history of working with bamboo but had never built full buildings out of it with curves. That was all something that my father started in the early 2000s,' explains Elora.

Bamboo is one of the most sustainable materials, for the simple reason that it's so quick to grow. Because its root structure is underground, bamboo poles can go from nothing to full maturity in three years — something that takes most timbers a generation to achieve. 'Each branch, each pole of bamboo is fully mature after three years, so you could build a house and, four years before, none of that material existed,' says Elora. 'It's just extremely sustainable.'

Echo House is a house that is very specific to its place — the owners of Echo House moved to Bali to be close to nature and so that their kids could grow up immersed in the jungle. The house offers that experience — it is open to the air and there is a sense of being immersed in nature, even within the house. The bamboo is part of that. The house communicates an affinity for nature, as well as being practically sustainable. Easy and quick to grow, bamboo is also strong and eventually biodegrades, going back to the earth.

Below: Other building materials include stone, glass and steel.

Following page: The bedhead, screen and ladder are all made of bamboo.

BAMBOO

Bamboo is a member of the grass family and there are more than 1400 species worldwide. It is very strong and has a growth cycle of three to five years, compared to ten to twenty years for wood. It also sequesters carbon from the atmosphere.

Echo House was built using bamboo construction methods developed by IBUKU and PT Bamboo Pure. IBUKU mostly uses the species *Dendrocalamus asper*, known as *petung* in Indonesia. The bamboo is purchased from hundreds of individual farmers, then treated with a salt solution to increase its longevity. At Echo House, bamboo was used in the construction of the house, including walls, floors, ceilings, screens, window frames, door frames and balustrades, as well as to build chairs, tables, light shades and other furniture.

Above: Bamboo furniture in the poolside kitchen.

Opposite: Copper shingles were used for the roof.

Deep retrofit with prefab extension

PROJECT	Low Energy House
LOCATION	Muswell Hill, London, UK
ARCHITECT	Architecture for London
BUILDER	Construction Hub
SITE AREA	700 m²
FLOOR AREA	195 m²
STOREYS	3
PHOTOGRAPHY	Lorenzo Zandri and Christian Brailey

The retrofit is mostly invisible in the old part of the house, including newly installed internal wood-fibre insulation.

SUSTAINABLE FEATURES

Airtight construction
Embodied energy reduction
Heat-recovery ventilation system
Lime plaster
Prefabricated structural
    insulated panel system (SIPS)
Triple-glazed windows
Wood-fibre insulation

When Ben Ridley, founder and director of Architecture for London, came across an Edwardian house that hadn't been renovated since the 1970s, he realised he'd found something special. Ben was looking for a home to renovate for himself and his family, but he also wanted the project to be an example of a sustainable retrofit of a typical London terrace on a constrained budget. The result is a meticulously crafted home that consumes considerably less energy than its neighbours, thanks to an insulated, airtight retrofit and an extension built with a prefabricated structural insulated panel system (SIPS).

Terrace or row houses are common in cities in the UK as well as other parts of the world. They have their challenges, including shared walls, lack of light and damp, but their original features often make them charming. When Ben found this home, it was unloved and suffering from damp and condensation issues, as well as mould, caused by cement-based renders and plasters trapping moisture. 'I bought the house with the goal of refurbishing it, so I was looking for an unloved home,' says Ben. 'The refurbishment celebrates the modest beauty and Edwardian character of the original building, while upgrading the materials that no longer served the house.'

The plan is straightforward, with the ground floor given over to one big living, kitchen and dining space. At the back, the extension creates extra floor space with a floor-to-ceiling window and timber-framed door offering views of a fern garden. The colour palette is restricted to white, grey and timber, with minimal detailing. On the floor above are three bedrooms and a bathroom, and the top floor loft extension has created space for two more bedrooms and a bathroom. The master suite features a sheer white floor-to-ceiling curtain across the bay windows that creates a sense of calm while allowing light to come in.

The house was renovated using natural materials, including stone, timber and lime plaster, which have less embodied energy than cement-based products. Lime plaster also creates an airtight layer that helps reduce heat loss in winter. A solid block of limestone was used for the kitchen island in the centre of the space, opposite a window seat, marking the social heart of the home. 'We used limestone for the island, creating a minimalist finish,' says Ben. 'We had never used this particular finish before. The slight polish means that it gently reflects light, and the way that light reveals the fossils in the stone is lovely.'

The rear extension was built using a structural insulated panel system that is relatively thin but highly insulated. The house is triple glazed with a continuous airtight layer and insulation to the entire building envelope. Walls were insulated externally at the side and rear, while internal wood-fibre insulation was used at the front of the house to retain the Edwardian facade. 'The aim is to create a continuous layer, like a warm jacket around the house,' says Ben.

With this level of airtightness, a heat-recovery ventilation system provides necessary preheated fresh air and also removes pollen, diesel particulates and other chemicals associated with air pollution.

Overall, it is the attention to detail across all aspects of construction that makes this home special. For example, the front door was retained but was made more airtight with simple do-it-yourself brush seals and a magnetic letterbox seal. 'People often think about sustainable design as expensive, but there are so many straightforward things people can do to make their houses greener that have meaningful results,' says Ben.

Embodied energy was also carefully considered, prompting design decisions that minimised energy expenditure. For example, in order to avoid using energy-intensive steel box frames on the ground floor, the architects instead chose to retain the masonry nib walls already in place.

Low Energy House, as it has been dubbed, was, in part, an exercise in demonstrating the simple steps it takes to retrofit a terrace house into an energy-efficient home that saves money on energy costs and provides a comfortable and healthy indoor environment, on a budget. The proof is in the numbers — after the retrofit, the house's heating costs were reduced by 80 per cent. But it is also a family home, one that Ben completed to his high aesthetic standards and that he says is 'delightful to come home to every day'.

The rear extension was
built using a highly efficient
structural insulated panel
system.

Top: The light colour palette includes white curtains that create a calm atmosphere.

Middle: The bathroom and both bedrooms feature electric underfloor heating.

Bottom: In the front living room, lime plaster has been added to existing brickwork.

Opposite: The kitchen island is a solid block of limestone.

Opposite: A built-in window seat beside the kitchen stairs looks out onto a garden.

Below: The new extension was built using a rendered structural insulated panel system.

STRUCTURAL INSULATED PANEL SYSTEM

Structural insulated panel systems (SIPS) are prefabricated panels made from an insulating core sandwiched between two faces, typically made of oriented strand board. They are precision-made in factory conditions to be thin, strong and airtight, and can be sized according to need, reducing waste on site.

At Low Energy House, a 172 mm structural insulated panel system was used for the rear extension. This system was chosen for its insulating properties, and has a Passive House-approved U-value of 0.15W/m^{2}K. It is cost-effective, due to decreased construction and labour costs, and results in a relatively thin wall.

Custodian of the waters

PROJECT	Tropical House
LOCATION	Tulum, Quintana Roo, Mexico
ARCHITECT	Jaque Studio
INTERIOR DESIGN	Daniela Parra
LANDSCAPE DESIGN	Rosario Ojeda
BUILDER	Jorge Kelleher
SITE AREA	2500 m²
BUILDING AREA	580 m²
STOREYS	1
PHOTOGRAPHY	César Béjar

This off-grid house is built
on one level and has a sloping
roof and clerestory windows
that face the pool.

SUSTAINABLE FEATURES

Battery
Chukum cement
Off grid
Onsite dark water treatment
Onsite well
Solar (30 kW PV array)

Set in a tropical rainforest in the Mexican town of Tulum, this sprawling single-level house is positioned to keep out the heat. It has large windows opening onto the gardens and an off-grid sustainable structure. The house is also oriented around water, with a cenote (natural waterhole), a new swimming pool and a natural wastewater treatment system.

Architect Jesús Acosta from Jaque Studio designed this house for a family of four who wanted to experience the beauty of nature within their new home. The 2500-square-metre site is on the outskirts of the town, on the flat landscape of the Yucatán Peninsula. Finding a site like this, with a gentle slope leading down to a small pond, is rare. Having studied the site, the architects decided that the house should be oriented towards this natural water feature, and that the building should not take up more than 40 per cent of the land. 'We [wanted to] preserve as much of the existing vegetation as possible and also respect the pond,' explains Jesús. 'Animals go to drink water from it and the continuous existence of water there means there's amazing vegetation.'

The placement of the house is one of the keys to its success. Rather than facing it south, as you normally would in the Northern Hemisphere, the architects considered just how hot this area is for most of the year and instead oriented the house to the north, which gets little sun, to also block out the harsh hot western sun. This also means the view is downhill, past the swimming pool to the cenote and the lush vegetation it supports.

Although the original brief could have been met with a one or two-storey house, the architects chose to keep the house on one level. Designed as a big L-shape, the layout of the house means each room has large windows that open to the jungle, so the residents never feel far from nature. 'When I was young, every time I went to the countryside to visit a friend's house for a weekend, I always remember just being in one-level houses,' says Jesús. 'It was very comfortable to move around, and you can move from one room to the other through the patio or corridor.'

One side of the L-shape is a long room with kitchen, dining and living spaces at one end and a courtyard garden and garage at the other. The other part of the L has a row of four main bedrooms that open onto the pool, and are connected to four oversized outdoor bathrooms — one each. 'Since we have an L-shaped floor plan, it's quite narrow. So we have cross-ventilation in every space of the house,' says Jesús.

The house mostly uses local materials to save money on shipping in materials from the USA or Europe. The base is made of a concrete slab and local stone, using the expertise of local stonemasons. It is low maintenance and provides structural support to help the house withstand hurricanes and other big storms. The upper layers are made mostly of timber and glass with finishes including limestone and chukum, a cement paste made with the sap of the chukum tree. Originally developed by the Mayans but lost after the Spanish conquest, the use of chukum in construction is now undergoing a revival in the Yucatán.

Sustainable services are extensive on this property. Solar panels with batteries mean that the house is not connected to grid electricity, although the orientation of the house and the use of passive solutions, such as cross-ventilation, means that there is little need to use air conditioning anyway.

Water is a big part of this site, and an important part of the house's architecture and systems design. The water for the house is drawn from the underground system then filtered to clean it and remove some of the minerals. Dark water is also cleaned on site and released back to the earth. The swimming pool adds to the water theme and is an idyllic place to take a dip.

Sustainable building solutions are becoming more cost effective and accessible the more they are implemented. Jesús says, 'The economies of scale are going to grow around that technology, and it's going to be more accessible for everyone.' On this site, the use of sustainable systems has created an off-grid home that makes the most of its jungle location.

A covered barbecue area is
tucked among the trees near the
living room end of the house.

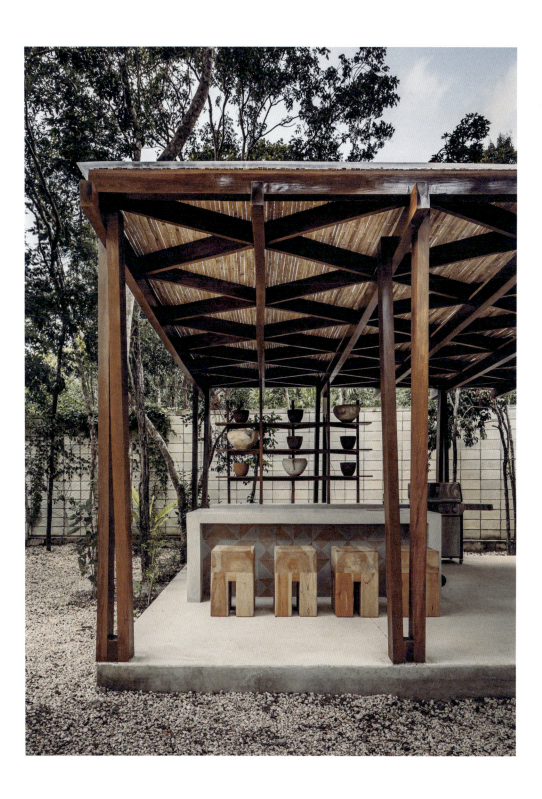

Opposite: Each bedroom has views of nature from the long strip balcony.

Right: The bathroom at the end of each bedroom is a private indoor—outdoor patio.

Following page: Most of the materials used in the main living space and kitchen were sourced locally.

Top: A treehouse nestles among the lush vegetation.

Middle: Timber is one of the key building materials.

Bottom: An additional outdoor dining space outside the northernmost living room.

Opposite: The whole property is off grid, with solar power and a battery, an onsite well and dark water treatment system.

WASTEWATER TREATMENT

Wastewater can be separated
into two types: greywater,
which is water from showers,
washing machines and sinks; and
blackwater, which is sewage from
toilets and dishwashers that
might contain solids. Treating
wastewater on site reduces the
volume of waste that is released
into the ecosystem and helps
reduce health hazards associated
with water pollution.

At Tropical House, dark water
is treated on site using a
wetland system that layers
it with vegetation and injects
the clean water back into the
underground water system.
The dark water is cleaned using
a biodigester — a sealed
container in which microorganisms
break down organic material
into biogas and fertiliser
through a natural process.

Opposite: View from the other
side of the pool where the land
slopes downwards.

Below: The main living room
has an open-air bathing room
with trees and a plunge pool-
style bath.

Sourced from the earth

PROJECT	Driemond House
LOCATION	Driemond, Amsterdam, The Netherlands
ARCHITECT	The Way We Build
BUILDER	The Way We Build
SITE AREA	440 m²
BUILDING AREA	100 m²
FLOOR AREA	135 m²
STOREYS	2
PHOTOGRAPHY	Tim Van de Velde

The architect-owner-builder created this prefabricated home with eco materials and a geothermal heat hump.

SUSTAINABLE FEATURES

CO_2 controlled mechanical
    ventilation
Geothermal heat pump
Laminated veneer lumbar
    ceiling beams
Prefabricated construction
Reclaimed tiles
Recycled textile roof insulation
Solar roof (80 x 6240 Wp
    PV panels)
Underground rainwater storage
    (1040 L)
Wood-fibre panel

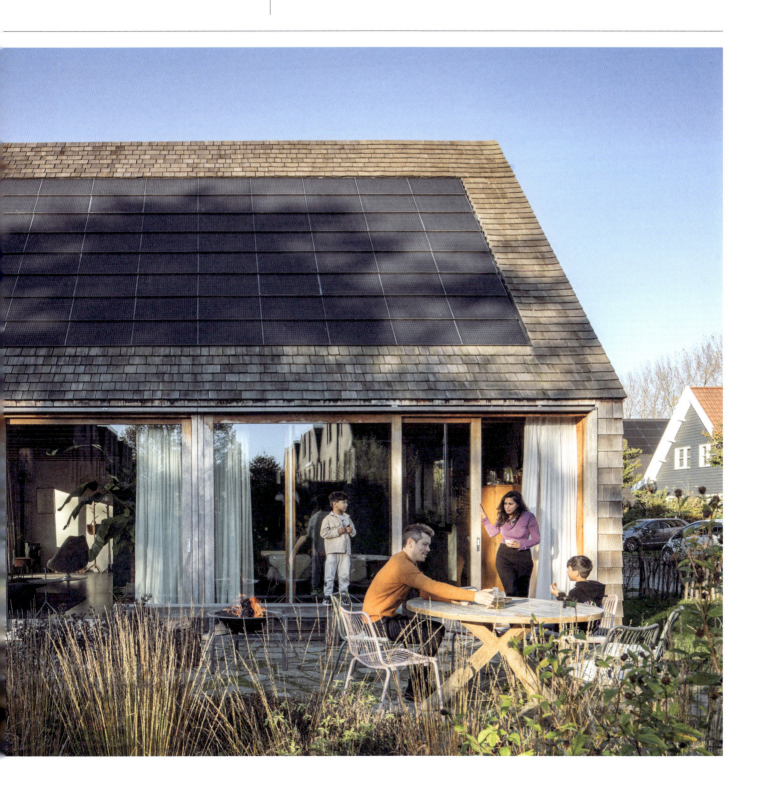

This house just outside Amsterdam was designed and built by Farah Agarwal and Arjen Aarnoudse from architecture studio The Way We Build for their small family. The house was constructed with prefabricated timber and has a garden inspired by the concept of rewilding. It also has an innovative source of heat — a geothermal heat pump that derives its heat from the earth.

Driemond House is part of a Dutch initiative that grants long-term leases to residents to build their own homes. Usually based on a lottery system, on this occasion, Farah and Arjen were given the pick of a few plots in a less-popular location past the last tram stop. They chose a corner plot to disrupt the usual row-house formation common in the Netherlands. The house faces north to capture the sunny southern aspect and offers views to the garden at the back. 'We have the south as garden space, and we made it so we can still walk around the house,' explains Arjen. 'Having this free feeling was very important for us.'

Zoning laws required the house to have a wooden facade. The sloping roof is also very Dutch, although the roof does not come to a point at the top the way dyke houses usually do. Farah and Arjen didn't see the need to create a loft space that would be basically unused, so the house has a flat roof instead. Otherwise, the house is simple in plan, with living spaces on the ground floor and bedrooms upstairs. On the ground floor, a bank of green joinery separates the kitchen from the living space, and there is also a built-in Murphy bed for visitors. The ground floor opens directly onto the garden. 'Every morning we open the curtains along the long curtain wall to have views to the garden,' says Farah.

The entire structure is made of Forest Stewardship Council (FSC) timber, and the main spruce frame was manufactured off site by a timber supplier in Latvia. The whole structure was designed and prefabricated, then shipped over by truck and assembled on site. 'It fitted perfectly,' says Arjen. The roof and walls are also timber, made from western red cedar shingles, and the window frames are untreated *Afzelia* wood. Inside, the ground-floor ceilings are made from laminated-veneer lumber, which was formed into long beams, strengthened by steel and left untreated so as not to introduce extra chemicals or need maintenance in future.

Gas is being phased out entirely in Amsterdam, so Farah and Arjen installed a new technology that is starting to gain traction — a geothermal heat pump. This technology uses the warmth of the earth to heat water, which is released into the floor of the house and used in the showers before being recirculated. Amazingly, the same system is used in reverse in summer to cool the house. The house also has solar panels, a charging station for a small electric car and a fireplace. 'On a cold winter's day or night, we gather around the wood-burning fireplace and drink hot chocolate,' says Farah. 'The fireplace is mostly for cosiness. We do not need it for warmth as the house is already always at a good temperature because of the excellent insulation.'

The materials in the house are also sustainable — not just the untreated internal wood, but also old tiles saved from other projects and insulation materials made of recycled cotton clothing that are very safe for builders to use. The green bank of joinery in the centre of the house is a wood-fibre panel made from recycled pine and mill waste, with all the wood fibres dyed to create a consistent green colour. There are no gutters on the house — the water runs off the roof, into a gutter on the ground that has pebbles on top, then into a reservoir under the car park. The family use it to water the garden.

Nature is also important in this project — the house is deliberately small to allow space for the garden, which feels wild thanks to asymmetrical paving and natural planting. The children play outside or go to the nearby dyke or the tiny forest that has been set up by the local community. 'The kids go out fishing, or play soccer or go to the horses in the back,' says Arjen. 'It's really outdoorsy, and we became outdoorsy because of the house.'

Driemond House is a model of a new way of building, giving residents the opportunity to construct their own home with sustainable materials and make something that's not about property values but about creating communities and opportunities to live in nature.

The ground floor living space
looks out to the garden.

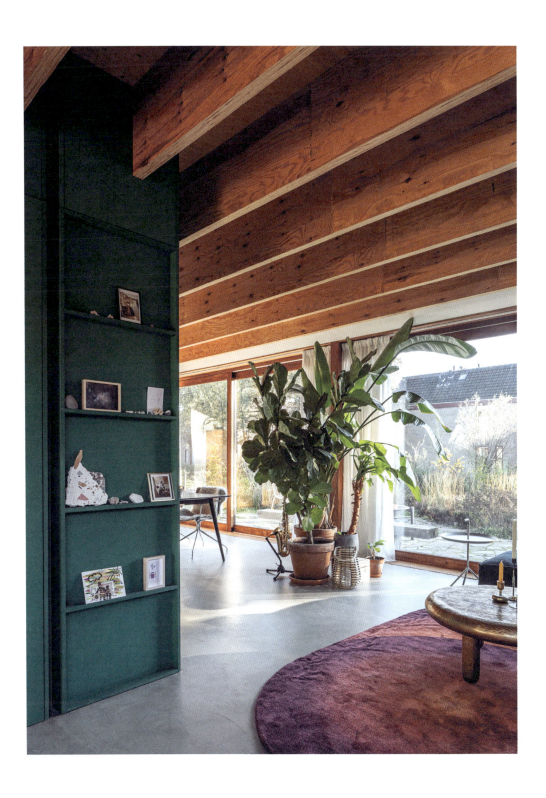

Top: This light's base is made
with reclaimed terrazzo.

Middle: The bathroom tiles,
and many of the other finishes,
came from leftover lots.

Bottom: The long ceiling beams
are made of engineered timber.

Opposite: The kitchen,
bathroom, stairs and Murphy
bed are all in a freestanding
green box.

Previous page: Dappled
light floods the living and
dining space.

Opposite: The garden is
designed to look a little wild.

Below: Heating, cooling and
hot water are generated with
a geothermal heat pump and
solar panels.

GEOTHERMAL HEAT PUMP

A geothermal heat pump sources
heat from the ground through
vertical water pipes. The
temperature of the ground remains
relatively constant all year
round, meaning that when water
is piped down into the earth
it is warmed in winter and cooled
in summer. The length of the
pipe or ground loop depends on
the size and usage of the home.
Once installed, it is a very
inexpensive way to heat and cool
a building.

At Driemond House, a geothermal
heat pump was installed with
two vertical 80-metre pipes that
extend down into the earth.
As well as providing heating and
cooling, the heat pump also has
an integrated hot-water heater.

Green to the core

PROJECT	Green House
LOCATION	Tottenham, London, UK
ARCHITECT	Hayhurst & Co Architects
BUILDER	Rebuild London
SUSTAINABILITY CONSULTANT	Mesh Energy
SITE AREA	295 m²
BUILDING AREA	110 m²
FLOOR AREA	189 m²
STOREYS	2
PHOTOGRAPHY	Kilian O'Sullivan

A translucent screen
creates a second, operable
skin for this house,
which is constructed from
cross-laminated timber.

SUSTAINABLE FEATURES

Airtight construction
Bamboo-planted facade with screen
Battery (12 kW)
Cross-laminated timber (CLT)
Embodied carbon: 373 kg CO_2eq/m^2
    (60-year lifespan)
Heat pump (air-source)
Prefabricated construction
Reclaimed concrete blocks
Recycled cork rubber
Solar (2.68 kW PV array)
Unfinished internal materials
Window insulation

This new two-storey house in Tottenham, north London, tackles sustainability with a holistic ethos. It incorporates a prefabricated cross-laminated timber (CLT) primary structure, sustainable materials and fossil-fuel-free energy. A carbon calculator was used to assess the embodied energy in the construction.

Situated on a block in Tottenham's Clyde Circus Conservation Area, Green House replaces a 1980s house that was poorly built in brick, with small windows, low ceilings and an awkward connection to the street. Nick Hayhurst and the team at Hayhurst & Co Architects first considered renovation rather than a new build, but found the old house was unworkable. 'I think our position was, if we are going to demolish it, then we have to make what we put back the best we can possibly do from a sustainability and environmental point of view,' says Nick.

The brief was for a family home for four that also had extra rooms for visiting family from France and the Netherlands. The owners wanted a home that felt connected to nature and had height to it — a sense of space. The budget was also a consideration in planning the method of construction. In response, the house was made of cross-laminated timber by a London company that fabricated the individual panels off site and assembled them on site in only ten days.

The timber is an Austrian spruce that, apart from a whitewashed fire treatment, was left untreated in the interiors, eliminating the need for plasterboard or plaster. Also, rather than building door frames and architraves, the frames were simply cut out of the walls, creating a seamless finish. 'We basically notched this cross-laminated timber to become the frame of the door, against everybody's advice,' says Nick. 'Everybody said, well, the timber might move a little bit, and then the doors might get a bit stuck. And one of them is a bit sticky. But it's been sanded and it's fine.'

The exterior cladding of the house is unusual too. At the front of the house, which faces south, a polycarbonate screen in front of a wall planted with bamboo creates a double-layer facade, filtering light, offering privacy and cooling the house on hot summer days. This facade also solves one of the biggest problems of the previous house, whose small windows meant that the front rooms became overheated to the point that Nick says it was 'almost unbearable'. 'Compared to what was there before, now you can actually be in the room with it quite open and the whole space feels quite cool and quite protected,' says Nick.

The layout of the house is a basic square. A central double-height space is surrounded by rooms on the ground floor and the level above, which are connected by a green-painted staircase in the centre of the void. Downstairs, the rooms flow freely from the kitchen to the double-height dining space through to the living space, where yellow and cream floor-to-ceiling curtains can be pulled across to create acoustic and visual privacy between the rooms. 'The curtains provide a level of adaptability in terms of being able to close spaces off [and] it partially helps absorption of sound,' says Nick. Even when pulled back and stored along blank walls, the curtains dampen the acoustics and bring vivid colour to the space.

The house is powered by a solar PV array and battery and is heated with an air-source heat pump. The home has a good level of airtightness and maintains a steady temperature of 21°C all year round. If the internal temperature gets too high, skylights controlled by temperature and rain sensors are opened automatically to provide ventilation. Some materials have been creatively repurposed from their intended use — agricultural roofing sheets are used as cladding, reclaimed concrete blocks have become pavers and cork that is normally used as a pipe insulation is flooring.

For Nick, who has always kept up with new sustainable developments, the next step is to calculate the embodied energy of a project, spurred on by new Royal Institute of British Architects targets for embodied carbon. Hayhurst & Co Architects now calculates the embodied energy in all its projects. At Green House, the embodied carbon was estimated using the Structure Workshop carbon calculator, providing guidance on best practice in the future.

Green House is an exemplar of prefabricated construction using a cross-laminated timber structure. It has just the right amount of light and privacy, planting to ensure healthy air and sustainable systems throughout — all on a relatively tight budget. Nick says, 'What's interesting about Green House is that its sustainability is not just applied, it's actually embedded within the strategy of what a building is in the first place.'

Below: Floor-to-ceiling
curtains create both acoustic
and visual privacy.

Following page: A green metal
staircase connects two storeys
through the central void.

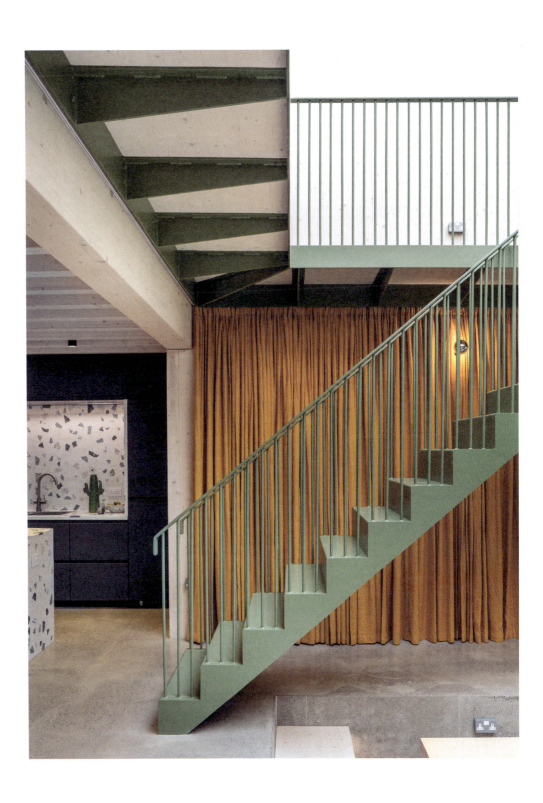

Top: Bamboo plants create
a green buffer between the
two layers of the facade.

Bottom: Seating space
in the middle of the house.

Opposite: Doors are cut
into the cross-laminated
timber walls.

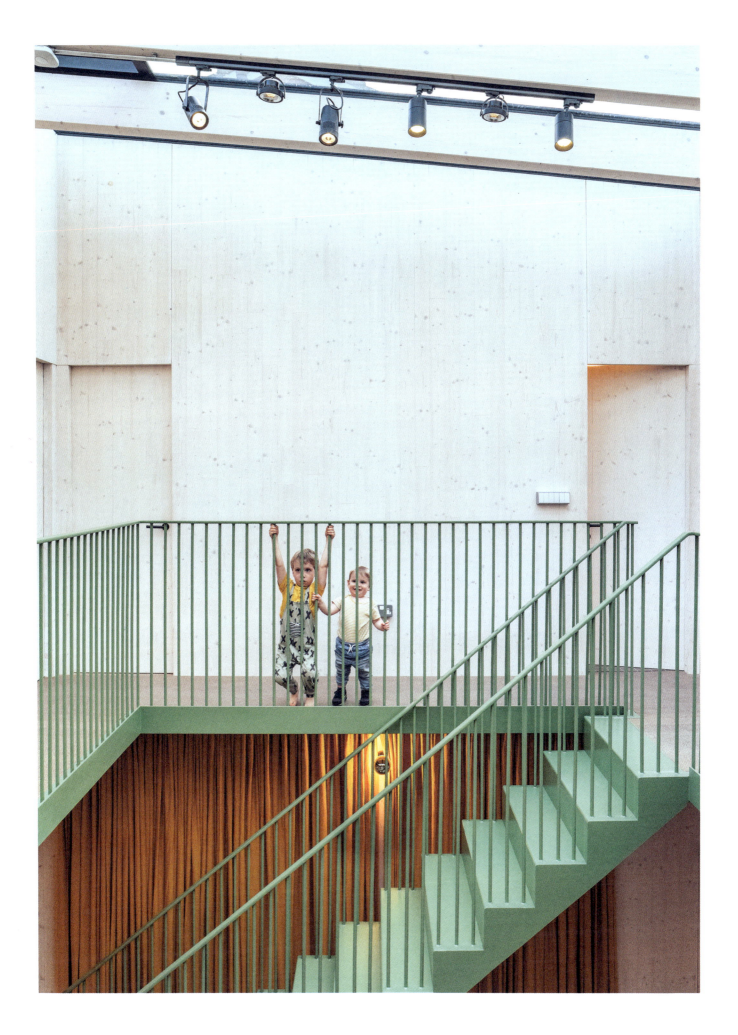

Opposite: In the main living space, the cross-laminated timber forms the walls and ceiling.

Below: Plants are everywhere in this house, even in the bathroom.

CROSS-LAMINATED TIMBER

The benefits of cross-laminated timber (CLT) are multiple — this engineered timber is both structural and visual, and because it is fabricated off site, can be constructed on site very quickly with minimal wastage. The timber used for CLT is fast-growing, can be treated to be fire-retardant and sequesters carbon during the building's lifetime.

At Green House, the CLT is a solid structural wall piece about 95 millimetres thick. Made from spruce, it only takes three seconds on a summer's day to grow the amount of CLT used in the house in the Austrian forests. Nick Hayhurst has been working with CLT for about thirteen years and, for this project, worked with a local London-based supplier.

Material advances with hemp

PROJECT	Flat House
LOCATION	Huntingdon, Cambridgeshire, UK
ARCHITECT	Material Cultures
BUILDER	Oscar Cooper, Henry Stringer, Simon Keeves, Jack Case, Brian Reid
SITE AREA	28 ha
BUILDING AREA	70 m²
FLOOR AREA	100 m²
STOREYS	2
PHOTOGRAPHY	Oskar Proctor

This house has prefabricated
hemp cassette internal walls
and hardened hemp and resin
sheet external walls.

SUSTAINABLE FEATURES

Battery (20 kW)
Carbon dioxide production:
    −2.2 t CO_2/year
Embodied carbon: −5.1 t
    (inc. sequestration)
Hemp fibre and sugar-based
    resin cladding
Prefabricated hempcrete cassettes
Solar (capacity for 6 kW
    PV array)
Unfinished internal materials

Flat House at Margent Farm is a family home for a filmmaker turned hemp farmer. Designed by experimental research practice Material Cultures, it sits on a former cattle farm north of Cambridge, UK. With 70 acres of land and a collection of barns, including one that had already been converted into a house, the site was the perfect place for a newly renovated family home and hemp farm. The owner sees hemp as a powerful tool in the fight against climate change due to its versatility as a material and ability to sequester carbon and this house is a powerful demonstration of biobased construction material. At Flat House, the architects used hemp to create a structural walling system as well as a corrugated cladding material made of hemp fibre and a sugar-based resin.

The new house makes the most of its south facade, with a wall of glass fitted into the existing steel frame that acts as a hothouse, capturing winter sun and reducing the need for heating in winter. Another steel frame has been retained as a pergola — in summer, the foliage of the deciduous climbing plants blocks out the hot sun, creating a dappled light effect. On the ground floor of the house is a large, open living, dining and kitchen space with a double-height ceiling. Two bedrooms tucked behind a wall have low ceilings that create a sense of cosiness and comfort. A staircase leads to a mezzanine above the bedrooms, where a large attic study or third bedroom leads out to a terrace.

The construction of the house was no ordinary feat. The house was built off site as prefabricated components — a kind of flat pack (hence the name Flat House) of hemp cassettes made of timber frames filled with hempcrete. This material remains exposed on the interior, creating a wonderfully tactile texture. 'The thing about building with natural materials is that they feel good to live with,' says architect Paloma Gormley. 'This experiential quality is something that, as architects, we can struggle to communicate the importance of.' On the exterior, hemp has been used in a different way, bound with a sugar-based resin and pressed into corrugated sheets. These are used to clad the building in the same way that a corrugated sheet metal would be. This new material was developed for this project and can now be purchased from Margent Farm.

Unlike conventional construction, where materials end up in landfill, both uses of hemp — interior and exterior — are not only biobased and therefore ultimately compostable but also non-toxic. They both create healthy indoor air quality and are better for the health of the builders who work with them. The dangers of working with asbestos are well known, but other building materials also have a detrimental effect on builders, plasterers and other tradespeople. 'The health impact of the construction materials that workers come into contact with on a daily basis is a massively under-reported issue,' says Paloma. 'Many of these materials are toxic and can do serious damage. Working with natural and biobased materials is a very different experience. They don't have this inherently negative impact on health.'

The walls have a high thermal mass, increasing the thermal capacity of the building. All power and heating is provided by a solar PV array and biomass. This house's energy efficiency is very high, scoring 102 out of a possible 104 in an energy performance test. Like other UK architectural practices, Material Cultures is tackling the issue of embodied carbon in their buildings. Flat House is carbon negative, after accounting for the biogenic carbon stored in the house.

Paloma views the oil economy, combined with globalised capitalism and the legacy of colonialism, as 'reaching this way of doing things that is highly extractive and irresponsible'. In response, she aims to combine contemporary modes of construction with more historic ways of doing things, rerouting architecture and construction in relationship to place, with 'shorter supply chains, more originally produced materials, a more direct relationship between where they come from and the buildings that they're applied to'.

Material Cultures was set up not just as an architecture practice, but as an organisation that is working towards a post-carbon built environment through research, education and advocacy. 'We teach in architecture schools and also run our own independent school called Material Cultures Make, which is about hands-on learning, working towards these skills and ideas being more accessible, and diversifying the construction industry,' says Paloma. This project serves as an example of how biomaterials such as hemp can revolutionise the construction industry — which is good for the environment and good for people.

Below: The existing structure
of the house was retained,
with glass installed to bring
in light.

Following page: Unfinished
hemp cassette prefabricated
wall panels in the kitchen-
dining space.

Above: View from a bedroom to
the main space and staircase.

Opposite: The unfinished
hempcrete creates an unusual
earthy texture.

HEMP FIBRE CLADDING

In construction, hemp is
traditionally used to create
hempcrete; however, new kinds
of hemp building products
that use hemp fibre are being
developed. Hemp is not only
a biobased material that is
biodegradable at the end of
its life, it also sequesters
carbon as it grows. When hemp
is put into a building, it stores
carbon, making it a carbon-
capture product.

At Flat House, the hemp fibre
cladding was developed by
Margent Farm's onsite research
and development facility, in
collaboration with the architects.
Unlike hempcrete, which is made
by combining hemp straw with water
and a lime binder, this product
takes the hemp fibre, binds it
with a sugar-based resin and then
presses it into corrugated sheets.
This new material can simply
be screwed onto battens, like
corrugated iron.

From freezing to fire

PROJECT	CAMPout
LOCATION	Lake Tahoe, Nevada, USA
ARCHITECT	Faulkner Architects
INTERIOR DESIGNER	Nicole Hollis
BUILDER	Jim Morrison Construction
SUSTAINABILITY CONSULTANT	Monterey Energy Group
SITE AREA	4187 m²
FLOOR AREA	333 m²
STOREYS	1
PHOTOGRAPHY	Joe Fletcher

External concrete and steel
walls protect this home from
extreme weather.

SUSTAINABLE FEATURES

Blown-in cellulose insulation
Radiant underfloor heating and
    hot water system
Underground rainwater storage

In the Sierra Nevada mountains, uncontrollable wildfires and very heavy snowfalls are increasingly becoming problematic. This new house by Faulkner Architects has been designed to withstand both extremes. Insulated concrete and blackened steel exteriors protect the interiors, a sheltered outdoor courtyard provides refuge in the centre of the home, and the roof is sloped to bring in southern sun in winter.

This four-bedroom home in the Sierra Nevada mountains, Nevada, was designed for a family that loves camping and mountaineering and wanted a retreat from their main home in San Francisco. Recognising the family's passion for the outdoors, Greg Faulkner and his team themed the house around camping, with the house acting as a 'base camp' for their next adventure. 'There's a campfire in the courtyard with wooden chairs around it. They can gather in the light of the fire, study their maps and plan their next trip,' says Greg.

Choosing a courtyard house plan was one of the big design decisions for this property. Although the house is on a slope, with views south to Lookout Mountain and north to the Martis Valley, it is still surrounded by neighbours, so the courtyard was about carving out a private sanctuary in the centre of the home. It is a way of accessing outdoor space while maintaining a hard edge that turns its back on the elements. It also allows breezes from the south and west to cool the home in summer.

Wildfires have increased in prevalence in this part of America and are now more common than ever before. Faulkner Architects is one of a number of architecture studios that are now designing houses to reflect that. In response to this risk, CAMPout has a concrete base with a mix of concrete and steel walls to the exterior around the edge of the home. These exterior materials reduce the risk of embers or burning vegetation setting the house alight. 'We just cannot build with wood anymore,' says Greg. 'There's just too much fire danger. The climate has changed. If you make a firm foundation out of concrete or stone, and then cap it with a steel plate roof, you're 90 per cent there, there's not much left to burn.'

Earth is also a great insulator. On the south, where the mountain slopes upwards, the house is nestled into the mountain face, with the roof nearly at ground level at the back where the bedrooms are.

The main living space, with large open living, dining and kitchen spaces, is in its own pavilion, made of concrete with a thin steel roof that slopes up to allow clerestory windows to bring in southern sun. The kitchen features uninterrupted black granite and steel, and has a smaller galley-style kitchen behind it for the stainless-steel appliances. The interiors have been designed to reflect the overall concept of a base camp. As just one example, a picnic-style dining table and bench seating lend the dining room the feel of a mountain cabin. 'The interior designer Nicole Hollis really reinforced the concept,' says Greg. 'She was meticulous in the way that the lighting, finishes and furnishings contributed to the shared concept.'

The house has been well insulated, with double eight-inch concrete walls filled with foam insulation that extends up to the roof and blown-in cellulose insulation. Materials reference the existing landscape, such as the basalt stone chosen for the flooring, and the unfinished native sugar pine used on the interior timber walls and ceilings. Extensive glazing has been limited to the courtyard to reduce fire risk, and smaller steel-sash tempered windows on the other exteriors form a fire-resistive barrier. As well as material considerations, the house has a radiant underfloor heating and hot water system, and the roof is designed so that rainwater flows from the gutters into underground stores.

Designing for wildfires and increased snowfall is a priority in this part of California and Nevada, and Faulkner Architects is continually working towards solutions. 'We use low, sloped roofs to keep the snow on the roof as insulation,' says Greg. '[We are] dealing with the cycle of winters and their severity, coupled with the results of that every year, in the summer and fall. The dry season is drier when [it is] preceded by a dry winter, and so forth. That's constantly something we have to gauge and build a defensive posture against.'

CAMPout is an insulated, robust structure, designed to reduce climate and fire risk, that uses local materials and sustainable systems to create the perfect 'base camp' holiday home.

The internal courtyard creates
a sheltered space that is open
to the sky.

From freezing to fire

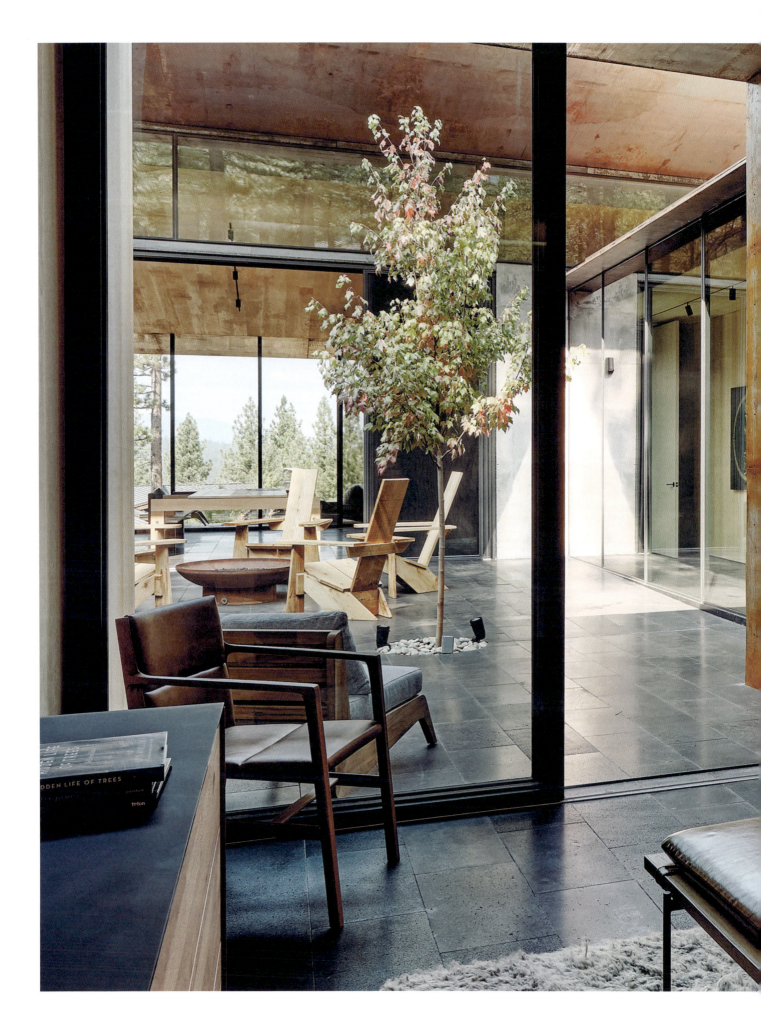

FIRE RATING

Fire activity is on the rise in many regions of the world, with recent devastating bushfires in areas including Australia, California, Portugal and Greece, as well as urban fires such as Grenfell Tower in the UK prompting a rise in the use of fire-resistant building materials. Steel, brick and concrete are some of the most fire-resistant materials, along with fire-rated glass and geobased materials such as mud brick.

For CAMPout house, steel and concrete block exteriors plus a steel roof were used to protect the house from fire, with more flammable materials like timber confined to the interiors. As a house usually first catches fire from embers on the roof or in a crevice or overhang, or from vegetation burning at the base of the house, the architects made sure to avoid flammable materials in these locations.

Previous page: Bedrooms circle the main courtyard.

Above: View of the forest and mountains beyond.

Opposite: In the event of a fire, there is no wood to burn on the exteriors.

House for woodworkers

PROJECT	HIÊN House
LOCATION	Hòa Quý, Da Nang, Vietnam
ARCHITECT	Winhouse Architecture
BUILDER	Winhouse Architecture
SITE AREA	105 m²
BUILDING AREA	74 m²
FLOOR AREA	350 m²
STOREYS	4 (plus rooftop garden)
PHOTOGRAPHY	Quang Dam

This home has a central void with a tree, and features recycled timber throughout the interiors.

SUSTAINABLE FEATURES

Green roof
Green verandas
Recycled timber

Situated in a suburb of Da Nang, near the Han River in Vietnam, this home was constructed from recycled timber by the three generations of woodworkers who now live in it. Built in a combination of traditional and contemporary styles over several storeys, the house is also dotted with gardens and planting that bring greenery into the home and onto its roof.

Although HIÊN House is in a part of Da Nang that has been newly developed, the family has a long connection with this part of Vietnam. They chose Winhouse Architecture because of their respect for this connection to a rural landscape, lifestyle and customs. Their brief was to incorporate elements of rural architecture into the urban environment. The key to this was the veranda — or *hiên* — a covered outdoor space.

The new house is a long, narrow building with three main floors and a smaller fourth floor, an atrium across all four storeys in the centre of the plan, and a sloping green roof. Inside the ground-floor entrance at the front of the house, a pond hints at a design that emphasises the natural world, while the interiors are largely dedicated to a large kitchen, dining and living space. On the level above are two bedrooms, each with a small bathroom, on either side of the atrium. Upstairs, the main bedroom with a veranda and outdoor bathtub is at the front of the house, and there is an open garden with another veranda at the back. On the half level above is a narrow study overlooking a garden at the front, and an altar and garden at the back, and the roof above also has its own garden space.

Most of the verandas are planted with foliage to create cool relaxing spaces to inhabit, each with a different amount of cover. The atrium and indoor gardens also give the feeling of verandas within the house itself — they are cool and leafy spots to feel the breezes and be in nature. '[The veranda] is not only an accent but also a traditional architectural feature that suits the tropical climate of Central Vietnam,' says Thai Huu Hai from Winhouse Architecture.

Green spaces are everywhere in this house — on each veranda over four levels, on the roof, and in the interiors. There is even a tree growing up through the atrium that has deep roots in the house's foundations. From the first-floor bedroom and bathroom at the front of the house, planting, in combination with a perforated facade, diffuses light and creates a soft, dappled effect. On the top floor, a creative studio space has a plant-filled box window that overlooks the green rooftop of the level below. The gardens are also functional, deterring pests and supplying vegetables and agricultural produce for the family to eat. Thai says, 'The design centres around the relationship between humans and nature. Green spaces establish a seamless connection between nature and daily activities.'

Although the house is constructed of several different materials, including concrete, concrete block, brick, plaster and terracotta roof tiles, the material that brings the home together, and makes it stand out visually, is timber. Timber framework, floors, window and door frames, screens and joinery, as well as built-in and freestanding furniture, have been crafted by the owners, who are woodworkers by profession. 'Woodworking has been passed down through generations, and it serves as the main inspiration for choosing wood as the primary material for this project,' says Thai.

Recycled timber salvaged from old buildings, such as schools and houses, was used to complete the structure, stairs and interior furniture of HIÊN House. In this part of the world, recycled timber is more cost-effective than freshly harvested wood. The family worked to bring out the colour of the wood, celebrating its natural characteristics without using chemical surface coatings. 'Both materials and labour are locally sourced, resulting in economic efficiency, environmental protection and ensuring the sustainability of this construction,' says Thai.

Vietnam has a tropical climate with warm weather all year round, so it is not necessary to insulate against cold. A bigger issue is Vietnam's fast-growing urban environments that do not have enough green outdoor spaces. Air pollution is also a major issue, which is why sustainable projects in Vietnam are about bringing greenery to the cities and suburbs. In HIÊN House, these issues are addressed by the creation of green spaces that also cool the house down. The use of recycled timber is also a major sustainable solution, reducing the need for virgin timber.

Below: Greenery cascades from
the verandas or *hieñs*.

Following page: Recycled
timber is used on walkways,
stairs, shelving, balustrades,
furniture and more.

Top: Shades on the skylight allow glimpses of the sky.

Middle: An outdoor bathtub on the terrace outside a third-floor bedroom.

Bottom: Timber was sourced locally from demolished buildings.

Opposite: Each floor is connected by timber walkways.

RECYCLED TIMBER

Using reclaimed timber has many environmental benefits, including reducing wood waste, limiting the felling of new trees (and accompanying deforestation) and fewer carbon emissions from material transportation. It is often as strong and durable as new timber, and can even be stronger and more stable. Timber is also better for the environment than many other interior finishes, especially petroleum-based carpet or linoleum.

At HIÊN House, the family's woodworking skills were a major factor in the decision to use recycled wood, as they were able to source the timber and also fit it into the home. The timber was salvaged from old schools and houses and reused, without any chemical surface coatings, to complete the roof structure, stairs and interior furniture. Materials and labour were both local, resulting in an economically efficient and environmentally friendly construction.

Above: This tiny office space at the top of the house has views of the rooftop garden.

Opposite: Indoor gardens create a veranda feel, even inside the house.

All natural
in the forest

PROJECT	Svinninge Cabin
LOCATION	Svinninge, Stockholm, Sweden
ARCHITECT	Lowén Widman Arkitekter
BUILDER	Martin Lydén
SITE AREA	779 m²
BUILDING AREA	102 m²
FLOOR AREA	176 m²
STOREYS	2
PHOTOGRAPHY	Erik Lefvander

This house in the forest
is made from cross-laminated
timber and is totally
petrochemical free.

SUSTAINABLE FEATURES

Airtight construction
Cross-laminated timber (CLT)
Double-glazed and
    triple-glazed windows
Heat pump and geothermal
    heat pump
Inner panels treated with
    beeswax, linseed oil
    and whiteboard pigment
Petrochemical free
Post and beam foundations
Underfloor hydronic heating
Unfinished internal materials
Wood-fibre insulation

This contemporary house built in a forest with traditional materials creates the perfect balance of rural charm and city convenience. Svinninge Cabin, a new build by Stockholm-based architecture studio Lowén Widman Arkitekter, was designed in line with Sweden's strict building codes, creating an energy-efficient home made for the climate. In addition to this, a respect for the land, a focus on quality and longevity, and the use of biobased materials — and importantly, no petrochemicals — makes this a stunning example of sustainable Scandinavian design.

The site for Svinninge Cabin was originally an empty plot. The owner-builder approached the architects with a plan to build a house they could sell after completion. As a result, the design is made to be flexible with a contemporary aesthetic that references traditional Swedish cabins. Although this was one of the first houses in the area, and the forest to the west is protected from development, the house is connected to grid electricity and water, and is only a short drive from the town centre and forty minutes to Stockholm.

The site is quite complicated and narrow but has the advantage of being on the edge of the forest with untouched woodland to the south and west. It also features many pine trees, including several that were protected, as well as a visible rock formation. Entry is from the road to the north of the site and the house was designed with an elongated floor plan running north to south. With neighbours to the north and east, these facades are relatively closed off for privacy, with small openings, but the western facade opens to forest views and afternoon sun. A long balcony on the ground floor runs the length of the house on the western side and is angled to avoid a protected tree to the north of the site and also create a connection with the forest to the south-west.

The wooden facades and gabled roofs on the exterior of the house are inspired by local housing. As the land falls away to the south, the house is raised on sawn spruce columns and its northern end sits on a slab. This serves two purposes: firstly, it avoids blasting the earth to create a level slab, and secondly, it allows nature to continue to exist underneath the house. 'We wanted to make nature able to grow under the house, so you could keep the blueberries, moss and a feeling of nature,' says architect Daniel Widman. 'Also, we wanted to avoid blasting. We wanted the house to adjust to the site and not the opposite.'

The construction is all timber — a stud frame, spruce cladding and engineered cross-laminated timber (CLT) inner walls, solid tongue-and-groove spruce flooring and ceilings, and larch door and window frames. Hydronic heating is used under the floors — for timber floors, it was placed in a groove in the chipboard beneath the timber. In Sweden, it is mandatory to insulate houses. A set formula mandates the size of windows, insulation levels, thickness of glass and airtightness, resulting in a highly sustainable solution. With Svinninge Cabin, the architects complied with these regulations but they also went one step further. They replaced the plastic and glass-fibre insulation commonly used in Sweden with a more natural, breathable wood-fibre insulation sandwiched between two layers of cross-laminated timber. 'Using plastic means when the cold air from outside meets the warm air from inside, there's a risk of condensation and black mould,' says Daniel. 'There's so many arguments to use no petrochemical materials.'

For Daniel, the sustainable measures mandated by Sweden are just part of doing architecture. His efforts to protect the land and use natural materials extend his sustainable practice, but there's also the question of longevity. 'I'm really against this low-quality, wear-and-tear, plastic society,' he says. He prefers to create architecture that is inspired by intelligent design from the past and built to last for generations to come. And then there is beauty. 'One of the most important things when it comes to architecture is beauty. It has to be nice and look good, because if it's nice and people who live there like it, then they will keep it and take care of it.'

It is easier to be sustainable when your country mandates energy efficiency and the protection of the natural environment as part of any new building, but there are always ways to improve on what everyone else is doing. Svinninge Cabin is a project that combines the basics with a close examination of every aspect of the build to create a contemporary, beautiful and natural home that is built to last.

Below: The spruce walls
and ceilings are made from
cross-laminated timber.

Following page: Swedish
building codes mandate
high levels of airtightness
and insulation.

Top: Even the kitchen bench
is made from engineered timber.

Middle: Built-in desk with
views of the forest.

Bottom: The bathroom features
large-format charcoal tiles.

Opposite: Plastic and glass-
fibre insulation was replaced
with breathable wood fibre.

PETROCHEMICAL FREE

The construction sector is one of the most polluting sectors on earth, and of the materials that can contaminate the environment, materials derived from petrochemicals are some of the worst. As well as being derived from fossil fuels, they have high embodied carbon and are virtually impossible to recycle at end of life. Walls, floors, insulation and siding can all contain petrochemicals and plastics, including PVC, which is often chosen as a lining material, and glass fibre-reinforced plastic insulation.

At Svinninge Cabin, the architects chose an all-natural timber construction method, but also considered all materials in the design of the building, purposefully making the choice to avoid any materials derived from petrochemicals. In particular, the usual plastic and glass-fibre insulation materials commonly used in Sweden were swapped out for a more breathable wood-fibre insulation.

Opposite: The house has space
for up to five bedrooms.

Below: Wood-fibre insulation is
sandwiched between two layers
of cross-laminated timber.

Following page: Large south-
facing windows in the living
room bring in winter light.

Architects

Altereco	altereco.net.au
Architecture for London	architectureforlondon.com
Austin Maynard	maynardarchitects.com
B.A.D	thebadstudio.com
DUST	dustdb.com
Faulkner Architects	faulknerarchitects.com
Hayhurst and Co Architects	hayhurstand.co.uk
Hé Architectuur	he-architectuur.be
IBUKU	ibuku.com
Jaque Studio	jaquestudio.com
Kennedy Nolan	kennedynolan.com.au
L'Abri	labri.ca
Lowén Widman Arkitekter	lowenwidman.se
Maria Milans Studio	mariamilans.com
Material Cultures	materialcultures.org
Melbourne Design Studios	melbournedesignstudios.com.au
Miquel Lacomba Architects	mlacomba.com
Nori Architects	norihisakawashima.jp
Of Possible	ofpossible.com
Paul Davidson	pauldavidson.nz
SJB	sjb.com.au
tono Inc	to-no.me
The Way We Build	thewaywebuild.com
Wardle	wardle.studio
Winhouse Architecture	winhouse.vn

Photographers

Anson Smart	ansonsmart.com
Casey Dunn	caseydunn.net
César Béjar	cesarbejarstudio.com
Christian Brailey	christianbrailey.com
Derek Swalwell	derekswalwell.com
Erik Lefvander	cargocollective.com/lefvander
Hinano Kimoto	hinanokimoto.com
Indra Wiras	indrawiras.com
Jade Cantwell	jadecantwell.com
Joe Fletcher	joefletcher.com
Junpei Suzuki	junpei-suzuki.com
Lorenzo Zandri	lorenzozandri.com
Maitreya Chandorkar	instagram.com/maitreya.chandorkar
Marnie Hawson	marniehawson.com.au
Mauricio Fuertes	mauriciofuertes.com
Montse Zamorano	montsezamorano.com
Noaidwin Studio	noaidwinsttudio.com
Oskar Proctor	oskarproctor.com
Quang Dam	quangdam.com
Raphaël Thibodeau	raphaelthibodeau.com
Rory Gardiner	rory-gardiner.com
Rui Nishi	
Simon Wilson	simonwilson.co.nz
The Fishy Project	thefishyproject.com
Tim Van de Velde	tvdv.be
Tommaso Riva	tommasoriva.com
Trevor Mein	trevormein.com
Wataru Aoyama	wataru-aoyama.com

Artwork credits

19 Waterloo Street by SJB	19: 20: 21:	*Morning Star Pole*, 2009, Gali Gurruwiwi Yalkarriwuy Bottom: *Eora*, 2022, Nicholas Harding *Banksia Grandis ceramics*, 2018, Cathy Franzi
Somers House by Kennedy Nolan	38: 39: 43:	Left to right: *Woven Bird* sculpture, date unknown, Tony Raguwanga Cameron; *Nude on Bed*, 2001, Mark Howson Middle: *Tiwi Island Totem* sculpture, date unknown, artist unknown; *Untitled*, date unknown, Mark Howson *Untitled*, 1992, Wayne Eager
Marfa Suite by DUST	50–51: 52:	Left to right: *Untitled*, Nick Terry, 2011; *Untitled*, 2019, Laszlo Thorsen-Nagel *Untitled*, 2020, Laszlo Thorsen-Nagel
Garden House by Austin Maynard Architects	70:	*Kosar Kursi* print, Joseph Au
HÜTT 01 PassivHaus by Melbourne Design Studios	112: 115:	Left to right: *Ordnung Muss Sein #6*, 2019, Richard Dunn; *Ordnung Muss Sein #1*, 2019, Richard Dunn; *Separation and Consolidation 1*, 2020, Ilona Herreiner *Redbank Gorge 1936 (after Albert Namatjira)*, 2002–2010, Richard Dunn
Puigpunyent Eco-Passive House by Miquel Lacomba Architects	121:	*Untitled*, 1989, Joan Lacomba
Anawhata House by Paul Davidson	134–135:	*Seated Nude* print, Carmel Van Der Hoeven
Karper by Hé! Architectuur	163:	Samples of earth plaster with algae, BC Materials
Bass Coast Farmhouse by Wardle	172–173:	*Warnarringa (sun)*, 2021, Dino Wilson, Jilamara Arts and Crafts
Flat House by Material Cultures	232: 234:	*I Am the One I've Been Waiting For* *(Red And Yellow)* art print, Harland Miller California Song, Hedi Slimane exhibition poster

About the author

Penny Craswell is an Australian writer based in Sydney with a Masters of Design from the University of NSW. She is the author of *Reclaimed: New homes from old materials* (2022) and *Design Lives Here: Australian interiors, furniture and lighting* (2020). A former magazine editor, Penny has curated exhibitions at the Australian Design Centre and Craft and Design Canberra, was Co-Director of Sydney Craft Week from 2017 to 2021 and contributes regularly to magazines around the world. Her essay 'On Cups' was published in the Penguin Random House anthology *Stories that want to be told* (2024). Her blog is The Design Writer.

Acknowledgements

Thank you to Thames & Hudson, especially publisher Paulina de Laveaux, who helped me choose the projects this time around, and editor Rachel Carter. Thanks to copyeditor Lorna Hendry for her excellent attention to detail and graphic designer Claire Orrell, whose designs never fail to impress. Thanks to all the architects and photographers whose work is featured. And thank you to my family, and especially to Chris, for all your wonderful support.

First published in Australia in 2024
by Thames & Hudson Australia
Wurundjeri Country, 132A Gwynne Street
Cremorne, Victoria 3121

First published in the United Kingdom in 2025
By Thames & Hudson Ltd
181a High Holborn
London WC1V 7QX

First published in the United States of America in 2025
By Thames & Hudson Inc.
500 Fifth Avenue
New York, New York 10110

ISBN 978-1-760-76401-2
ISBN 978-1-760-76477-7 (U.S. edition)

 A catalogue record for this
book is available from the
National Library of Australia

British Library Cataloguing-in-Publication Data
A catalogue record for this book is available from
the British Library

Library of Congress Control Number 2024939735'

Aus edition front cover:
HÜTT 01 PassivHaus by Melbourne Design Studios
Photographed by Maitreya Chandorkar, Marnie Hawson

US edition front cover:
Tropical House by Jaque Studio
Photographed by César Béjar

Back cover:
Flat House by Material Cultures
Photographed by Oskar Proctor

Camp O by Maria Milans Studio
Photographed by Montse Zamorano

Design: Claire Orrell
Editing: Lorna Hendry
Printed and bound in China by C&C Offset Printing Co., Ltd

MIX
Paper | Supporting
responsible forestry
FSC® C008047

Thames & Hudson Australia wishes to acknowledge that Aboriginal
and Torres Strait Islander peoples are the first storytellers of this
nation and the Traditional Custodians of the land on which we
live and work. We acknowledge their continuing culture and pay
respect to Elders past and present.

Be the first to know about our new releases,
exclusive content and author events by visiting

thamesandhudson.com.au
thamesandhudson.com
thamesandhudsonusa.com